Literature Search Strategies for Interdisciplinary Research

A Sourcebook for Scientists and Engineers

Edited by
Linda G. Ackerson

D0557906

THE SCARECROW PRESS, INC.
Lanham, Maryland • Toronto • Plymouth, UK
2007

SCARECROW PRESS, INC.

Published in the United States of America
by Scarecrow Press, Inc.
A wholly owned subsidiary of
The Rowman & Littlefield Publishing Group, Inc.
4501 Forbes Boulevard, Suite 200, Lanham, Maryland 20706
www.scarecrowpress.com

Estover Road
Plymouth PL6 7PY
United Kingdom

British Library Cataloguing in Publication Information Available

Library of Congress Cataloging-in-Publication Data

Literature search strategies for interdisciplinary research : a sourcebook for scientists and engineers / edited by Linda G. Ackerson.
    p. cm.
  Includes bibliographical references and index.
  ISBN-13: 978-0-8108-5241-9 (pbk. : alk. paper)
  ISBN-10: 0-8108-5241-1 (pbk. : alk. paper)
  1. Interdisciplinary research—Methodology. 2. Research—Methodology. I. Ackerson, Linda G.

Q180.55.I48L58 2007
507.2—dc22   2006021534

∞™ The paper used in this publication meets the minimum requirements of
American National Standard for Information Sciences—Permanence of Paper
for Printed Library Materials, ANSI/NISO Z39.48-1992.
Manufactured in the United States.

Contents

Preface

Linda Graves Ackerson was an exemplary engineering and science librarian and scholar, specializing in collection development, instruction, and user services. Her particular areas of expertise were user information seeking behaviors and information resources for interdisciplinary research. She published several prominent papers in these areas and this book on interdisciplinary research support provides a fitting capstone to her career.

Linda was dedicated to her work. Even when she was physically unable to work, she continued to pour her energy into editing this book and refining the introduction and her chapter. Linda strongly believed in the importance of this book and would have been proud to see it in print.

Linda touched many lives in her professional work and her personal contacts with library patrons, colleagues, and the graduate assistants (library school students) that we train in the Grainger Engineering Library. Linda was particularly proud of the success of our former graduate assistants who now serve in library positions all around the world. She greatly enjoyed talking and meeting with them at professional meetings and hearing from them as their careers unfolded. Linda's legacy lives on in these former graduate students whenever they use a collection development tool or electronic reference resource that they were trained to use by Linda.

In 2004, Linda was tenured as associate professor of library administration. The university and library honor faculty who receive tenure by having them select a book which is inscribed with a bookplate that describes how

v

that title has influenced their life. Linda selected "To Kill a Mockingbird" by Harper Lee. Her bookplate reads:

> I grew up in rural Alabama, and this book captures the essence of my childhood. Atticus Finch demonstrates the best qualities of humanity: honesty, respect, and courage. I read this book again every year, because it gives me hope about our world.

Linda very much exemplified these virtues: honesty, respect, and courage.

William H. Mischo and Mary C. Schlembach

Introduction

The purpose of this book is to help scientists and engineers plan a successful search strategy to achieve a thorough literature search. The book will be most useful for beginning scientists and for researchers who are moving from a broad disciplinary research area to a more specialized field. The volume of published literature is overwhelming, particularly in fields that use information from more than one discipline. Interdisciplinary research areas are known as "high scatter" fields, because useful information can be found within the publications scattered across many disciplines.[1] Interdisciplinary research requires a well-formulated question for multiple disciplines to join and pursue the solution to a real-life problem. Without a focused inquiry, the researcher may find too little information or may be overwhelmed by too much.

Because the terms interdisciplinary, multidisciplinary, and cross-disciplinary are used interchangeably, it is useful to define these concepts. The following definitions are based on those of Julie Thompson Klein.[2] The term interdisciplinary describes an integrative process in which knowledge from two or more distinct disciplines is synthesized to form a new field. Multidisciplinary research is an additive process in which information from multiple disciplines is used. Cross-disciplinary research is the sharing of information across disciplines. Whereas interdisciplinary research often results in the formation of a new field, the other two types use the combined knowledge of multiple disciplines, often to solve specific problems, but seldom create a stable field.

Academic disciplines differentiate themselves by the objects they study (e.g., fossils); the methods they use to study the objects (e.g., x-ray diffraction); and concepts (e.g., creation of structures at the atomic level).[3] Any classification system used to divide and order scientific knowledge will be somewhat arbitrary. Time and progress erode distinct boundaries. However, scientific knowledge can generally be organized into five classic categories:

1. Physical sciences (e.g., astronomy, chemistry, geology, physics)
2. Mathematics (e.g., statistics and probability)
3. Life sciences (e.g., biology, medicine)
4. Applied sciences (e.g., computer science, engineering)
5. Social sciences (e.g., anthropology, economics, education, psychology)

Fields are defined as stable, self-sustained research areas formed by the combination of two or more disciplines. These areas are supported by specialized societies and organizations, conferences, and publications, which provide forums for the exchange of information among scientists in many disciplines. Newly emerging fields are still in the process of identifying the fundamental principles that caused their division from parent disciplines.[4]

Effective search strategies help to organize the literature and make it easier to locate pertinent information. The following ten chapters examine specific inter-disciplinary fields and illustrate the information needed to shape a strategy. The authors of these chapters have extensive experience working in academic science and engineering libraries and are skilled in designing complex literature searches. The chapters are arranged in chronological order, beginning with the oldest.

Individual research, experimentation, and informal observations may occur over decades before the information is available to other scientists. The firm age of the field is difficult to establish but was resolved to be set at the approximate date when there was evidence of formal discourse or written communication on the subject area (i.e., the point at which publications in the field were most likely to first appear). Three factors were used to reasonably determine the birth of the field: the date the first specialized journal or book was published, the date the first specialty organization was formed, or the date the first conference convened.

The crux of creating a step-by-step strategy to search for literature in interdisciplinary fields is to know what questions to ask. Here are the four key questions and the methods by which the questions may be answered:

1. Which subject areas should I search?
2. How far back in time should I search?
3. How is research in the field disseminated?
4. Which basic sources should I use to find the most important publications?

The first step is to learn more about the field. Specialized encyclopedias are good introductory sources, because they focus on the history and development of the field, including its birth date (if known), and the primary disciplines involved in its formation. Specialized encyclopedias also outline main topics of research. The philosophy of the field can be found in classic texts, and annual review series can be used to closely trace the development of the field over time. The history and development of the field helps answer the first two questions. *WorldCat*, a composite source of worldwide library catalogs, is a good source for identifying books by subject.

Guides to the literature and bibliographies outline the type of sources by which the literature in a field is organized and identify important, seminal publications. Some selections are the Butterworths Guides to Information Sources series; the Engineering Literature Guide series, compiled by the American Society for Engineering Education; and the LC Science Tracer Bullets series, produced by the Library of Congress.[5] Although many of the Tracer Bullets research guides are dated, the structure of the literature and seminal publications in each subject change little over time. New Tracer Bullets are created by the Library of Congress Science Reference Services when newly emerging areas are recognized or by demand from scholars. The LC Science Tracer Bullets are online at www.loc.gov/rr/scitech/tracer-bullets.

CHARACTERISTICS OF INTERDISCIPLINARY RESEARCH

A number of similarities are revealed across interdisciplinary fields. First, it is not always possible to credit the birth of a field to just two parents. Many fields utilize the knowledge, techniques, and tools of several disciplines to develop their individualities.[6]

U.S. government documents are important sources of information in most research areas. Scholars in atmospheric chemistry depend on data gathered by the Environmental Protection Agency and the Department of Energy. Much of the pertinent information in bioethics is contained in the U.S. judicial literature as written policies, acts, and court decisions. Information on patents, crucial in the practice of engineering entrepreneurship, is available from the U.S. Patent and Trademark Office.

Fields are sustained through the organization of specialized societies or associations. Prior to the establishment of specialized societies, research in the field is presented at the conferences of parent disciplines. Early work in some fields was carried out at conferences, which attract scientists from many disciplines and provide opportunities for discussion of common interests. For example, computational biologists attend conferences sponsored by the Association for Computing Machinery and the American Medical

Informatics Association (AMIA). The International Society for Computational Biology originated from meetings held at the Intelligent Systems in Molecular Biology conferences in the early 1990s. Conference proceedings may be the first place that research in a newly developing field is published prior to its appearance in peer-reviewed journals. Therefore, conference proceedings are a significant source of information in many fields.

Research centers are common in interdisciplinary studies. The Hastings Center was crucial to the growth of bioethics research, because it was an established site where scientists could meet and voice concerns about bioethical topics. The Hastings Center also published the first journal in the field. Some centers, like the Foresight Institute, acted as a clearinghouse for collecting and disseminating information on nanotechnology. Collaborative research between universities and industries occurs in such centers to develop innovative products.

For interdisciplinary literature searching, it is necessary to search for information in more than one source. There is no central subject index; disciplines have their own primary indexes. Diversity in searching is especially necessary when the literature search involves a field created by a combination of physical science and social science disciplines. Pertinent information in human factors engineering will be found in both engineering and psychology publications. Developing a search strategy for this field is complex because the structures of their literature greatly differ. The most important psychological literature is in the form of journal articles. Primary literature in engineering can be published as journal articles, technical or government reports, or in statistical form.

In order to plan a successful search, the searcher must be familiar with the indexing policies of secondary sources (i.e., print and electronic indexes). The indexing policy is a profile of coverage based on the following variables: subjects, range of years from which citations are drawn, types of materials included, and geographic areas covered. Some fields have more than one primary index, so all should be searched because of indexing policies.

A good example is the comparison between the two major indexes for finding earth sciences literature. The databases *GeoRef* and *GEOBASE* both cover the subject areas of agriculture, anthropology, environmental studies, geography, and geology. *GEOBASE* also covers oceanography, geomechanics, and ecology. *GeoRef* allows one to search for literature published from 1732 to the present by using both the print and electronic indexes. *GEOBASE* coverage is from 1980 to the present. *GeoRef* includes citations to journal articles, books, conference proceedings, reports, theses, and maps, while *GEOBASE* indexes only journal articles. Both currently provide international coverage, but geographic areas outside North America were only covered back to 1933 in *GeoRef*. *GEOBASE* offers slightly more width in subject coverage. Other variables—like the date ranges covered and inclusion of literature from other parts of the world—are different between the two databases. To perform a complete search, both sources in print and electronic formats should be examined.

CHAPTERS SUMMARIES

Summaries of the subject areas illustrate the common themes of interdisciplinary research described above. The unique features of the fields are also characteristic of interdisciplinary research.

Chapter 1: Paleontology

Paleontology was formed by the interaction of biology and geology. Scientists from these two disciplines study fossils for different reasons. Biologists are interested in the evolution of the plants and animals prior to fossilization. Geologists study fossils as a record of past environments in which the organisms lived. The disciplines are linked because they both use biological nomenclature to classify organisms. The first book to include information on fossils was *De Natura Fossilium*, published in 1546.[7] It is an important book, because it was the first book to include illustrations, which allowed new specimens to be compared with others to see if they were already classified or if the specimen was a new, uncataloged species.

The first specialized journal was not published until 1807. Books published before then influenced advancement of the field more than the journal literature. The literature of paleontology is valuable after many years, based on biological nomenclature, which never goes out of date.

Chapter 2: Crystallography

In 1723, Moritz Cappeller published the earliest treatise on Crystallography, titled *Prodromus Crystallographiae de Crystallis Improprie sic Dictis Commentarium*, which marks the beginning of the field.[8] Pioneering research in crystallography was done simultaneously by scientists in physics, chemistry, geology, and mathematics. The results of that research were first published in the journals of those disciplines. The first journal devoted exclusively to crystallography was published in 1877.

Some fields experience birth as a precipitate event, while others evolve more slowly. Modern crystallography became an independent field in 1912 with the discovery of x-ray diffraction, a tool that could be used to discern molecular patterns in solid substances. The discovery became a milestone in science because it could be used in the research of so many areas. However, years of research literature had preceded this date back to 1723. Some fields, like crystallography, are the result of a clearly defined event, such as x-ray diffraction.

Chapter 3: Quaternary Research

Quaternary research is the product of the disciplines biology, chemistry, anthropology, geology, and geography. Russia formed the first International Association for Studying the Quaternary Period of Europe in 1927. In 1928, the International Union for Quaternary Research was founded by a group of scientists already involved in interdisciplinary research on environmental changes. The first congress of this organization convened that same year. Today, approximately ten organizations sustain Quaternary research as an independent field, and the author rates networking with other scientists as one of the most important resources in the field.

One of the unique features of Quaternary research is the field's considerable use of "grey literature." Grey literature is defined as "that which is produced by government, academic, business, and industries, both in print and electronic formats, but which is not controlled by commercial interests and where publishing is not the primary activity of the organization."[9] Field trip guidebooks, for example, are difficult to obtain, because the guidebooks are sometimes held only by the trip participants.

Chapter 4: Human Factors Engineering

Human factors engineering is primarily a mixture of engineering and psychology. The field focuses on the design of man-machine systems. Military research centers were established in the mid-1940s, and much of the early literature was published in the form of government documents that reported on the results from government-sponsored projects. The first human factors engineering formal organization, the Ergonomics Research Society, formed in 1949 in Great Britain as a forum for scientists from all disciplines—physicists, psychologists, physiologists, physicians, and engineers—to discuss common interests.[10] However, knowledge from the field was soon applied to civilian activities in industry beginning in the 1960s.

The *Human Engineering Bibliography* was compiled by Tufts University in a series of volumes.[11] The purpose of the series was to gather citations to all literature published in journals, laboratory reports, government documents, and other types of sources. Volume 1 of the series covered literature published from 1950 through 1955. From this bibliography, the date of the field was set at 1950, when the first published literature was reported.

Subject terms change over time, between disciplines, and across geographic areas. Human factors engineering illustrates all three conditions.

As an example of how subject terms can vary by location, the concept is termed "human factors" in the United States, but "ergonomics" in Great Britain.

These problems can be controlled with time and specialized interdisciplinary vocabulary. Problems with finding older literature are common in many fields. Human factors engineering is a good example of how to overcome this problem by using a subject thesaurus to identify correct keywords and authorized subject headings. Reading about the history and development of human factors engineering is useful in determining that the first civilian application was in industrial engineering in the production and distribution of goods.

The major index for locating engineering literature is *Compendex*, the electronic equivalent to *Engineering Index*. Both *Compendex* and *Engineering Index* coverage goes back to 1884. No thesaurus of authorized subject headings for this index was published until 1990, so researchers had to look for keywords throughout the print volumes. That far back, only broad subject terms, not keywords, were assigned to index entries by the Engineering Information staff when the index was written. To find literature on human factors engineering from 1918 through 1939, researchers would have to know that the broad heading of industrial engineering had the most relevant keywords and look for the following subject terms: industrial management, industrial psychology, industrial welfare, and human engineering.

The thesaurus for engineering literature has been updated several times to accommodate changes in concepts and terminology. In 1990, the thesaurus *SHE: Subject Headings in Engineering* was published. *SHE* was updated by *Ei: Engineering Index* in 1993. Use of the thesaurus leads the researchers to additional new subject headings, such as engineering psychology, human factors, and human engineering.

The primary index to finding psychology literature is *PsycINFO*. The basic electronic index covers material back to 1967, and the thesaurus is part of the search software. The equivalent print index, *Psychological Abstracts*, covers material from 1927. The *Thesaurus of Psychological Index Terms* is the thesaurus for the print index. The researcher should search for the following terms in the older volumes: applied psychology, engineering psychology, human factors engineering, computer-assisted design, and human engineering.

Chapter 5: Nanotechnology

The field was formed from the disciplines of physics, chemistry, and engineering. The seminal publication is the transcript of a speech given by Richard P. Feynman at the annual meeting of the American Physical Society on December 29, 1959. A transcript of the talk was included as a chapter in the book *Miniaturization* in 1961.[12] This chapter received 104 citations between 1961 and 2005.

Feynman believed miniaturization was not yet possible in 1959, because no instrument was sophisticated enough to see individual atoms. The invention of the scanning tunneling microscope, invented in 1981, could see individual atoms of conductive material. The atomic force microscope, invented in 1986, could see individual atoms in nonconductive materials. Although the invention of the two microscopes defined the field, an extensive body of literature has been generated on nanotechnology since 1961, and this date has been set as the birth of the field.

The *Science Citation Index* is contained in the commercial group of citation databases known as *Web of Science*. The citation indexes are unique sources of information for all categories of science, because they allow searching for pertinent articles cited by relevant authors.

Chapter 6: Atmospheric Chemistry

The parent disciplines of this field are geology and chemistry. The first specialized journal was published in 1962. Atmospheric chemistry is of immense interest to the public because it involves environmental issues such as ozone, air quality, and greenhouse gases. Three main societies— the American Chemical Society, the American Meteorological Society, and the American Geological Union—support atmospheric chemistry as one of its divisions. The societies advocate for additional government standards for environmental issues studied by this field.

Atmospheric chemistry shows how the support of U.S. government funding and professional organizations affects progress in many scientific fields. Most of the atmospheric data is collected by equipment, such as aircraft, satellites, and ground instruments, purchased through U.S. government grants. The National Oceanic and Atmospheric Agency gathers information on oceans, atmosphere, space, and the sun. The Aeronautics and Space Administration picks up information on Earth's radiation, clouds, and aerosols.

In addition to funding research, government agencies distribute information on reports and statistical data gathered in the projects. The U.S. Environmental Protection Agency distributes information on radiation, radioactive materials, fuel economy, acid rain, climate protection, and air quality. The U.S. Department of Energy Carbon Dioxide Information Analysis Center has created a database of information on subjects such as levels of carbon dioxide and other gases in the atmosphere, long-term climate trends, and the impact of rising sea level on coastal areas.

Chapter 7: Bioethics

If pressed, the disciplines of biology and medicine can be considered the foundation of bioethics. However, the "ethics" portion of bioethics is defined by the inclusion of theology, philosophy, and law. The date of the field's inception has been set at 1969, when the Hastings Center was established. The first specialized journal in bioethics was published in 1971 by the Hastings Center.

While most of the other fields experience problems when searching across disciplines, bioethics shows the complications at the highest degree. With multiple disciplines in both the categories of life and social sciences, a major question is knowing how far back to search the literatures of these five disciplines. It is useful to know the span of time over which research articles are still useful to current experimentation. For example, the information on philosophy maintains its usefulness for a long time. Research in medicine and biology, on the other hand, ages very quickly. Also, as the authors point out, it is imperative to search for articles and other materials in multiple indexes, especially for fields of controversial nature, to get alternative viewpoints.

Chapter 8: Computational Biology

This field was created from the disciplines of biology and computer science, with contributions from research in medicine and mathematics and statistics. The precipitating events that supported the separation of this field from its parents were the simultaneous announcement of sequence data on the human genome. At the same time, the Internet allowed the data to be widely disseminated to other scholars. Computational biology researchers develop algorithms and computational tools to store, search, and analyze data. The age of the field was set by an article published in 1970 about the development of a sequence assignment algorithm to help process the huge amount of data open to other scholars.[13] From 1970 to 2005, the article has been cited 288 times in other papers, per *Science Citation Index*, and began the flurry of published literature on the Human Genome Project.

Many scientific and engineering disciplines depend on data sets posted on the Internet to advance their research. Computational biology is a prime example of the importance of open access to reports of the sequence data gathered by many researchers and shows how the data can be organized for more efficient use. Although Internet websites are a crucial part of the knowledge network in these fields, they are cited infrequently in the book. Data from one site may be moved to another without advance notice, URLs change, or the sites may not be curated. Therefore, only official government and association websites are cited.

Chapter 9: Engineering Entrepreneurship

Engineering entrepreneurship is the product of business and engineering. The age of the field's inception was set at 1970, with the establishment of the first entrepreneurship center at Southern Methodist University. Shortly afterwards, entrepreneurship was added to the university degree fields and scholarly study. Education in this area prepares business and engineering schools to collaborate in management and technology.

A unique feature of this field is the inclusion of patents as an important part of the structure of the field's primary literature. Because new technologies are used to design and construct new products and processes for commercial purposes, intellectual property is an important issue.

Chapter 10: Machine Learning

Some fields emerge gradually, while others emerge as the result of a definitive event, such as the discovery of x-ray diffraction. Machine learning did not become a separate area of research for at least three decades after the concept was envisioned in 1950. Machine learning demonstrates that fields are not always the offspring of only two disciplines and are dependent on the progress in related fields. Machine learning especially thrives on the research and progress of artificial intelligence. There is some doubt about whether machine learning was born as an independent field or whether it is a subfield of artificial intelligence.

NOTES

1. Marcia J. Bates, "Learning about the Information Seeking of Interdisciplinary Scholars and Students," *Library Trends* 45, no. 2 (Fall 1996): 156.

2. Julie Thompson Klein, *Interdisciplinarity: History, Theory, and Practice* (Detroit: Wayne State University Press, 1990).

3. Alessanadra Cancedda, "Concepts and Relationships between Disciplines (paper presented at XIII World Congress of Sociology, Rome, Italy, 1994), 2–4.

4. Bates, "Learning about the Information Seeking of Scholars and Students," 156.

5 Michelle Cadoree Bradley, e-mail conversation, May 20, 2005.

6. C. B. Duke, "The Birth and Evolution of Surface Science: Child of the Union of Science and Technology," *Proceedings of the National Academy of Sciences of the United States of America* 100, no. 7 (April 2003): 3, 858–64.

7. Georg Agricola, *De Natura Fossilium*, trans. Chance Bandy and Jean A. Brandy (New York: Geological Society of America, 1955).

8. J. Lima-de-Faria and others, eds., *Historical Atlas of Crystallography* (Boston: Dordrecht, 1990), 6.

9. Pat Sulouff and others, "Learning about Grey Literature by Interviewing Subject Librarians," *College and Research Libraries* 66, no. 7 (July/August 2005): 511.

10. Frederic Bartlett, "Bearing of Medicine and Psychology on Engineering," *Chartered Mechanical Engineer* 8, no. 5 (May 1961): 297–99.

11. Tufts University Institute for Applied Experimental Psychology, *Human Engineering Bibliography*, 6 vols. (Washington, DC: Office of Naval Research, Department of the Navy, 1959).

12. Richard P. Feynman, "There's Plenty of Room at the Bottom," in *Miniaturization*, ed. Horace D. Gilbert (New York: Reinhold Publishing, 1961), 282–96.

13. S. B. Needleman and C. D. Wunsch, "A General Method Applicable to the Search for Similarities in the Amino Acid Sequence of Two Proteins," *Journal of Molecular Biology* 48, no. 3 (March 1970): 443–53.

1

Paleontology

Ron Gilmour

Sir Charles Lyell (1797–1875) defined paleontology as "the science which treats of fossil remains, both animal and vegetable."[1] This definition points directly at the dichotomy that makes this field interdisciplinary. On the one hand, animals and vegetables are the legitimate business of the biologist, while their "fossil remains" are found within the realm of the geologist. Paleontology is generally thought of as a subdivision of geology or the earth sciences, and paleontologists in universities are most often members of such departments, although a few are situated in biology departments.[2] The literature follows the same trend. Textbooks and historical surveys of geology will generally contain a full chapter on paleontology, while works on biology rarely contain such chapters, instead discussing fossils within the larger context of evolution.

To expand further on Lyell's definition, we must examine the problematic term "fossil." Derived from the Latin *fossilis*, "dug up," this term was originally used to describe almost anything found in the ground, including man-made items and unusual rocks or crystals. The term was popularized by Georg Agricola in his *De Natura Fossilium* of 1546.[3] Since the nineteenth century, it has been used more narrowly to describe the organic remains of animals or plants, although it can also be used to describe "trace fossils," such as the tracks or burrows of animals.[4]

The field of paleontology may be subdivided in various ways. The most obvious division is between animals and plants, yielding the subfields of paleozoology and paleobotany, respectively. In practice, the term paleozoology is little used, since paleontology is often assumed to deal with animals. Another division is based on the split between biology and geology.[5] Researchers whom we might call geological paleontologists are interested in fossils primarily for the light that they shed on questions of stratigraphic correlation or on the nature of ancient environments. Conodonts, paleozoic toothlike fossils, for example, were used as indicator fossils of stratigraphic importance long before their biological nature was established. They are now considered the remains of a primitive vertebrate. Biological paleontologists, or paleobiologists, are more concerned with the organisms than with their remains: their evolution, phylogenetic relationships, ecology, and even behavior. In practice, paleobiology is used almost synonymously with paleontology except that the former excludes biostratigraphy.[6] Within the realm of invertebrate paleontology, the geological tendency is often dominant, while vertebrate paleontologists seem to take a special delight in imagining the lives of the organisms that they study.[7]

HISTORY AND DEVELOPMENT

The earliest records of stones that resemble organisms are from the ancient Greeks. Some Greek thinkers, including Pythagoras and Herodotus, accepted fossils as the remains of formerly living organisms, while others, including Aristotle, regarded them as the products of spontaneous generation (or what Aristotle's student Theophrastus called a *vis plastica*) within the earth.[8] The Aristotelian view remained common throughout the Middle Ages and Renaissance and survived in some quarters until the seventeenth century. Robert Plot (1640–1696), in his 1676 *Natural History of Oxfordshire*, described fossil shells as being the product of "some extraordinary plastic virtue latent in the earth."[9]

An alternative to the spontaneous generation of fossil forms by mysterious forces in the earth was to regard the fossils as the actual remains of the organisms that they so closely resembled. This created the problem of accounting for the occurrence of seashells on mountaintops and in inland locations. The biblical flood provided a plausible mechanism for such amazing transports, and Christian writers as early as Tertullian (ca. A.D. 155–ca. 222) embraced this theory of fossil origins. The English physician John Woodward (1665–1728) championed this viewpoint in an essay published in 1695. Such theories did not disappear entirely until the nineteenth century.[10]

A convenient starting point for the history of paleontology in a modern sense is the Swiss naturalist Conrad Gesner's (1516–1655) book *De Rerum Fossilium Lapidum et Gemmarum* (1565). This was the first book on fossils to make use of illustrations.[11] This was an important advance over Agricola's book, as it allowed future readers to form hypotheses about the objects that Gesner described. High-quality illustrations have continued to play a vital role in paleontology to the present day. Gesner had intended this small volume as a prelude to a larger work, but he succumbed to the plague shortly after its publication. Gesner was primarily concerned with describing and illustrating the objects that he collected and did not comment directly on their origins.[12] The Italian naturalist Fabio Colonna (1567–1650) was among the first to explicitly relate fossils to living organisms. He figured fossil and extant mollusks together in his works and wrote an essay in 1616 asserting that the fossils known as *glossopetrae* were the actual teeth of sharks. He still faced the problem of how these came to be embedded in rock and could only fall back on biblical flood theories.[13] Similar observations about the teeth of sharks were made independently by the Danish physician Niels Stensen (better known as Steno, 1638–1687) when he dissected a shark in Florence in 1667.[14]

Robert Hooke (1635–1703), perhaps best known as the father of microscopy, took up the question of fossils in the chambers of the Royal Society in London. Hooke had already published his *Micrographia* (1665), in which he demonstrated the close resemblance between fossil wood and charcoal. He argued for the organic nature of fossils based on the philosophical observation that if the form of a shell is related to its function of protecting a living animal, to suppose that a form so closely similar arose in the absence of an animal to protect was incompatible with an orderly universe.[15] Opponents of Hooke's view included the physician and mollusk specialist Martin Lister (ca. A.D. 1638–1712) and the German Jesuit Athanasius Kircher (1602–1680), who maintained that fossils resulted from a plastic force within the rock.[16] They, and others who doubted the organic origin of fossils, argued that since some fossil species differ significantly from any living species, they could not originate from a living organism. The notion of extinction was viewed as antithetical to the idea of a perfect world designed by a perfect Creator. English naturalist John Ray (1627–1705) attempted to circumvent this problem by proposing that living analogs to fossil species might still exist in unexplored parts of the earth.[17] An interesting middle way between the organic and inorganic theories of fossil origin was proposed by Edward Lhwyd (1660–1709) of the Ashmolean Museum in Oxford. Cognizant of microscopic discoveries of reproductive particles such as sperm and pollen, Lhwyd suggested that fossils did form within the rocks as Aristotle believed, but that they did so not in response to a *vis plastica* but rather as a result of contact with the "seed" of living organisms on the earth's surface. Ray found this theory attractive, although he was concerned that it still did not address the problem of species extinction.[18]

Our history to this point has favored England, but Hooke and Ray were not succeeded by naturalists of a comparable stature, and the Royal Society of London went on to claim its greatest victories in the realms of mathematics and the physical sciences rather than the earth or life sciences. It was left to the Frenchman Georges-Louis Leclerc, Comte de Buffon (1707–1788) to summarize the state of geological knowledge in the first volume of his *Histoire Naturelle* of 1749.[19] (He was obliged, however, by pressure from the church, to recant many of his views on the formation of the earth.[20]) The next great steps in paleontology were taken by de Buffon's countryman George Cuvier (1769–1832), the father of comparative anatomy and perhaps of modern paleontology.

Cuvier was a professor of anatomy at the newly founded Musée National d'Histoire Naturelle in Paris. He began his work at the age of twenty-five alongside such future luminaries as Jean-Baptiste de Lamarck (1744–1829) and Etienne Geoffroy Saint-Hilaire (1772–1844).[21] Cuvier was a vertebrate anatomist by training and was among the first to use the techniques of comparative anatomy to determine the nature of fossil organisms.[22] His first great accomplishment lay in proving the reality of extinction, specifically in relation to extinct pachyderms and the *Megatherium*, a giant ground sloth. His views on the *Megatherium* were presented to the public in a lecture at the National Institute of Sciences and Arts in Paris, and perhaps marked the beginning of the paleontologist's status as a public figure.[23] Cuvier's later research continued to produce descriptions of fantastic extinct creatures. His discoveries made him famous not only in scientific circles, but also among amateurs. The French public's appetite for spectacular, extinct monsters was apparently equal to that of twentieth-century Americans. Cuvier's public success may also be attributed to the fact that the secularism of post-revolutionary France made the concept of extinction less controversial than in England.

Cuvier's older colleague de Lamarck, however, argued that the nonexistence of a giant ground sloth in the present did not necessarily prove the extinction of the species. The *Megatherium* may have undergone transmutation into a new, extant form. In nineteenth-century France, extinction and evolution were seen as diametrically opposed theories to account for the absence of living mastodons and ground sloths.[24] De Lamarck's research on the invertebrate fossils of the Paris region ultimately led him to adopt the view that species evolved over time, a theory to which Cuvier objected vehemently.[25]

One of Cuvier's strangest discoveries was an animal that combined features of the rhinoceros, pig, and tapir. He named the creature *Palaeotherium*, noting that it came from sediments older than most of his previous discoveries. This inspired his general observation that the fossil fauna found in older strata are more different from extant animals than are the fossils in recent strata.[26]

Much of Cuvier's later work on the chalk formations surrounding Paris was accomplished in collaboration with Alexandre Brongniart (1770–1847). This work was historic in that it set a precedent for using fossils to define particular strata within a formation, thereby emphasizing the importance of paleontology for stratigraphic studies.[27] Brongniart's son Adolphe (1801–1876) became one of the founding figures of the science of paleobotany with his *Histoire des Vegetaux Fossiles* of 1828.[28]

In England, William Smith (1769–1839) was already using stratigraphic techniques similar to those used by Cuvier and Brongniart.[29] Smith is often named alongside Cuvier and de Lamarck as one of the fathers of modern paleontology.[30] The views of Smith and Cuvier were popularized in England by Robert Jameson (1774–1854) and William Buckland (1784–1856), both geologists with theological leanings. They tried to correlate stratigraphic chronology with biblical narrative, once again raising the specter of Noah's flood in scientific discourse.[31]

The late nineteenth century was a time of intensive fossil collecting and systematizing. The British Museum (Natural History) and the American Museum of Natural History became important centers of research and repositories of paleontological collections. Spectacular finds of this era included the protobird *Archaeopteryx* from Germany, and many Jurassic dinosaurs from the western United States.[32]

The publication of Darwin's works in the mid-nineteenth century gave a new context to paleontological studies, although a surprising number of paleontologists were hostile to Darwin's theory of natural selection. Many favored neo-Lamarckian viewpoints in which "inherent trends" and "laws of development" directed evolutionary progress, rather then the reproductive success of organisms possessing advantageous, randomly generated variations.[33] These non-Darwinian viewpoints account for some of the common iconography associated with paleontology, such as the linear sequences of increased body size and toe fusion in the lineage of the modern horse and the famous linear ascent from ape to human.[34]

Since the beginning of the twentieth century, paleontology has begun to address broader questions. New fossils continue to be found and described, and the evidence that such discoveries bring to bear on the evolutionary history of life on earth is examined in the literature. But there is also a trend toward more holistic views of fossil history resulting in the fields of paleoecology and paleobiogeography.[35] Paleoecology attempts to reconstruct what ancient environments may have been like and how their members interacted.[36] Paleobiogeography tracks "the distribution of the various forms of life, over the earth, in past geological times."[37] This science contributed important evidence to the emergence of plate tectonics in the 1960s by showing that very similar fossil assemblages occurred on land masses that are not presently contiguous.[38] Studies in both of these fields are informed by the field of paleoclimatology, which aims to reconstruct the climate of past ages.

STRUCTURE OF THE LITERATURE

As in the other natural sciences, the journal article is the primary unit of dissemination for paleontology. Books, conference proceedings, government documents, and textbooks are also important sources of information. The trend toward preprint servers that is evident in some of the physical sciences has not yet emerged in paleontology, perhaps due to the importance of high-quality photographs and illustrations in this field.

Early research was published in general scientific journals such as the *Annales des Sciences Naturelles* in France and the *Philosophical Transactions of the Royal Society of London* in England. American paleontologists published in the *Transactions of the American Philosophical Society, Proceedings of the American Academy of Arts and Sciences,* the *American Journal of Science, Proceedings of the Boston Society of Natural History,* and the *Proceedings of the Academy of Natural Sciences of Philadelphia.*

In the nineteenth century, more specialized journals appeared. Among the earliest journals specifically devoted to paleontology were the German journals *Zentralblatt für Geologie und Paläontologie* (began 1807; fossil studies comprised its "Teil II") and *Palaeontographica* (began 1846). The latter journal is divided into two series, the first covering paleozoology and stratigraphy and the second devoted to fossil plants. By the end of the nineteenth century, there were also specialist journals in France (*Mémoires: Paléontologie;* began 1890), Switzerland (*Abhandlungen der Schweizerischen Paläontologischen Gesellschaft;* began 1874), Italy (*Bullettino di Paletnologia Italiana;* began 1875), and the United States (*Bulletin of the American Museum of Natural History;* began 1881).

From 2000 to 2004, the top five current journals in paleontology were *Palaeogeography, Palaeoclimatology, Palaeoecology; Geology; Nature; Palaios;* and *Journal of Human Evolution.*[39] The fact that fossil fuels (mostly the remains of carboniferous trees) are the industrial world's major energy source means that governments and corporations may be intensely interested in paleontological discoveries. This is especially true in the United States, where the U. S. Geological Survey (USGS) is an important producer and distributor of geological information. Not only does the USGS publish paleontological findings in their monograph series, professional papers, and reports, but they also serve as the major source for geologic maps, which are vital to the work of any paleontologist. The USGS website (www.usgs.gov) serves as the major entry point to this organization's vast resources. This site includes a search engine of USGS publications back to the survey's origin in the late nineteenth century. A history of the survey is also available on this site.

Paleontological literature does not go out of date. J. Nudds and D. Palmer analyzed the references of papers in four major paleontological journals as well as *Nature.* They found that for three of the paleontology journals (*Ge-*

ologica et Palaeontologica, Journal of Paleontology, and *Palaeontology*), about ten percent of references were to materials published prior to 1910. Less than two percent of citations in *Nature* and *Paleobiology* were for pre-1910 materials. The researchers attributed this difference to the fact that the first group of journals was more taxonomically oriented.[40] As in the fields of botany and zoology, paleontologists often consult the first description of a particular organism. This is particularly important when there is a question of correct nomenclature, since biological nomenclature works on a rule of priority. Often, a new specimen must be compared to a published description to see if it falls within the scope of a known organism's variation or if it must be named as a new species.

SEARCHING THE LITERATURE

The major bibliographic databases for the geological sciences in general are *GeoRef* and *GEOBASE*. *GeoRef,* produced by the American Geological Institute, is more narrowly focused on the geological sciences and goes back much further in time, while *GEOBASE* is more interdisciplinary and has a fairly shallow time scope.

GeoRef is the best starting point for most serious searches of the paleontological literature. It corresponds to the print sources *Bibliography of North American Geology, Bibliography and Index of Geology Exclusive of North America, Geophysical Abstracts, Bibliography and Index of Geology,* and *Bibliography of Theses in Geology. GeoRef* contains over two million records, dating back to 1785 for North American material and 1933 for the rest of the world. It covers not only journal articles, but also books, conference proceedings, and government documents.

GEOBASE is more interdisciplinary in scope, covering environmental sciences, geography, and oceanography as well as geology. Its coverage extends back only to 1980. Searching *GEOBASE* can be a useful supplement to searching *GeoRef,* as it seems to be updated more frequently so that newer papers may show up in *GEOBASE* first. Because of the difference in temporal scope, a search in *GeoRef* will almost always yield more records than the same search in *GEOBASE.* However, there will often be an article or two (often not from the United States or United Kingdom) in *GEOBASE* that will not show up in the *GeoRef* search.

Because paleontology is an interdisciplinary science, searches of the geological literature should be supplemented by searches of the biological resources. This is truer for some types of organisms than others. In the field of paleobotany, for instance, it is common for fossil studies to be published alongside papers on extant plants in journals such as the *Botanical Journal of the Linnean Society* and the *American Journal of Botany.* General journals on mollusk biology, on the other hand, seem less likely to publish paleontological papers. Searches of *Biological Abstracts* are useful, but results will often largely overlap a similar search done in *GeoRef*. Again, the differences will often be in materials published in countries other than the United States and United Kingdom. The database *Zoological Record* should also be consulted for searches involving animal fossils. When the remains of early man or questions of hominid evolution are involved, the *Anthropological Literature* database should be consulted.

A number of print reference sources are useful to paleontologists. An excellent guide to these sources is Ann Lum's chapter in *Information Sources in the Earth Sciences*.[41] Lum offers an overview of general reference works and textbooks as well as sections on major resources related to certain themes (e.g., phylogenetics, origin of life, paleoclimatology) and groups of organisms. One useful work for general reference that postdates Lum's synthesis is the *Encyclopedia of Paleontology*.[42] This two-volume encyclopedia contains authored articles on many aspects of paleontology as well as biographical articles on prominent paleontologists. The articles contain lists of references and suggestions for further reading. Also noteworthy is the expansive textbook *Paleobiology: A Synthesis*.[43]

NOTES

1. Sir Charles Lyell, *Elements of Geology* (London: J. Murray, 1838), quoted in John Challinor, *A Dictionary of Geology*, 3rd ed. (Cardiff: University of Wales Press, 1967), 180.

2. Bernhard Zeigler, *Introduction to Palaeobiology: General Palaeontology* (Chichester, England: Ellis Horwood Limited, 1983), 1.

3. J. C. Thackray, "History of Palaeontology: Before Darwin," in *Palaeobiology: A Synthesis*, ed. Derek E. G. Briggs and Peter R. Crowther (Oxford: Blackwell Scientific Publications, 1990), 537.

4. John Challinor, *A Dictionary of Geology*, 3rd ed. (Cardiff: University of Wales Press, 1967), 256.

5. Karl von Zittel, *History of Geology and Palaeontology* (Weinheim, Germany: J. Cramer, 1962), 363.

6. Challinor, *A Dictionary of Geology*, 178.

7. See Martin J. S. Rudwick, *Scenes from Deep Time: Early Pictorial Representations of the Prehistoric World* (Chicago: University of Chicago Press, 1992).

8. W. N. Edwards, *The Early History of Palaeontology* (London: Trustees of the British Museum (Natural History), 1967), 1–3.

9. Edwards, *The Early History of Palaeontology*, 5.

10. Edwards, *The Early History of Palaeontology*, 11–12.

11. Thackray, "History of Palaeontology: Before Darwin," 537.

12. Martin J. S. Rudwick, *The Meaning of Fossils: Episodes in the History of Palaeontology*, 2nd ed. (New York: Science History Publications, 1976), 1–9.

13. Rudwick, *The Meaning of Fossils*, 42–44.

14. Thackray, "History of Palaeontology: Before Darwin," 538.

15. Rudwick, *The Meaning of Fossils*, 53–56.

16. Rudwick, *The Meaning of Fossils*, 56–64.

17. Thackray, "History of Palaeontology: Before Darwin," 539.

18. Rudwick, *The Meaning of Fossils*, 84–86.

19. Rudwick, *The Meaning of Fossils*, 93.

20. O. C. Marsh, "History and Methods of Palaeontological Discovery" (address delivered before the American Association for the Advancement of Science, Saratoga, NY, August 28, 1879), 17.

21. Rudwick, *The Meaning of Fossils*, 101–2.

22. Marsh, "History and Methods of Palaeontological Discovery," 21–22.

23. Rudwick, *The Meaning of Fossils*, 105–9.

24. Rudwick, *The Meaning of Fossils*, 115–19.

25. Marsh, "History and Methods of Palaeontological Discovery," 25–26.

26. Rudwick, *The Meaning of Fossils*, 124–27.

27. Thackray, "History of Palaeontology: Before Darwin," 540.

28. Henry Andrews, *The Fossil Hunters: In Search of Ancient Plants* (Ithaca, NY and London: Cornell University Press, 1980), 64–66.

29. For a popular account of Smith's career and his famous geologic map of England, see Simon Winchester, *The Map that Changed the World: William Smith and the Birth of Modern Geology* (New York: HarperCollins, 2001).

30. For example, Marsh, "History and Methods of Palaeontological Discovery," 22; and Edwards, *The Early History of Palaeontology*, 38.

31. Thackray, "History of Palaeontology: Before Darwin," 541–42.

32. P. J. Bowler, "History of Palaeontology: Darwin to Plate Tectonics," in *Palaeobiology: A Synthesis*, ed. Derek E. G. Briggs and Peter R. Crowther (Oxford: Blackwell Scientific Publications, 1990), 543–44.

33. Bowler, "History of Palaeontology: Darwin to Plate Tectonics," 545–46.

34. For more about the iconography of progressive evolution, see Stephen Jay Gould, *Wonderful Life: The Burgess Shale and the Nature of History* (New York: W. W. Norton & Co., 1989), 27–45.

35. J. W. Valentine, "History of Palaeontology: Plate Tectonics to Paleobiology," in *Palaeobiology: A Synthesis*, ed. Derek E. G. Briggs and Peter R. Crowther (Oxford: Blackwell Scientific Publications, 1990), 549–50.

36. See papers in Anna K. Behrensmeyer and others (eds.), *Terrestrial Ecosystems through Time: Evolutionary Paleoecology of Terrestrial Plants and Animals* (Chicago: University of Chicago Press, 1992).

37. Challinor, *A Dictionary of Geology*, 178.

38. Bowler, "History of Palaeontology: Darwin to Plate Tectonics," 547.

39. A more complete list of major journals in paleontology is given in J. Nudds and D. Palmer, "Societies, Organizations, Journals, and Collections," in *Palaeobiology: A Synthesis*, ed. Derek E. G. Briggs and Peter R. Crowther (Oxford: Blackwell Science Publications, 1990).

40. Nudds and Palmer, "Societies, Organizations, Journals, and Collections," 524–25.

41. Ann Lum, "Palaeontology," in *Information Sources in the Earth Sciences*, ed. David N. Wood, Joan E. Hardy, and Anthony P. Harvey, 2nd ed. (London: Bowker-Saur, 1989), 236–73.

42. Ronald Singer, ed., *Encyclopedia of Paleontology* (Chicago and London: Fitzroy Dearborn Publications, 1999).

43. Derek E. G. Briggs and Peter R. Crowther, eds., *Paleobiology: A Synthesis* (Oxford: Blackwell Scientific Publications, 1990).

2

Crystallography

Gregory Youngen

Crystallography is the science of examining the structure of materials on the atomic scale. This includes defining the molecular structure, identifying all the atoms present along with their spatial patterns, and establishing correlations with a substance's physical and chemical properties. Counting the number of neighbors around an atom and measuring the distances between their centers from diffraction patterns provides basic information on the structure and properties of elements and compounds. Research based on crystallographic data, or employing crystallographic techniques, is core to the fields of chemistry and solid state physics and is of immense importance in such diverse areas as biotechnology, pharmaceutics, genomics, semiconductor research, nanotechnology, materials science, and metallurgy.

Originating in the field of mineralogy, crystallography's fundamental theories are based on atomic physics and mathematics. Its importance to chemistry and biology was soon realized by providing a method for explaining how the atomic structure of a material determines its physical properties, and in the process, leading to an understanding of chemical and biological events.

Today, applications of crystallographic research cross the boundaries of all conventional scientific disciplines. The techniques employed in crystallography continue to expand our knowledge of the physical, chemical, biological, and materials sciences by providing detailed structural analysis of solid state organic and inorganic compounds, and more recently, vitamins, proteins, and polymers.

The use of x-ray crystallography to determine the structure of DNA is acknowledged as one of the milestones of twentieth-century science; and more recently, fullerene chemistry, high-temperature superconductors, and the design of antiviral AIDS medications are among the areas in which crystallography has played a vital role.

This chapter will provide an overview of the information needs in crystallography and review the major print and electronic resources in the field. In addition, an attempt will be made to demonstrate the symbiotic relationship between advances in the pure and applied sciences and the correlating developments in the field of crystallography.

CRYSTAL STRUCTURE

Crystals are geometrically ordered and constitute a state of matter in which the atoms are arranged in regular patterns. The most distinguishing characteristic of a crystal is that it is based on some repeating pattern of atoms. The fundamental data about crystal structure are concerned with a description of the nature of this pattern: its symmetry and the way the pattern is repeated in space.

Alan L. Mackay notes a crystal structure may be viewed as a repetition in space of some elementary unit.[1] A lattice is used to describe such ordered structures. Graphite is soft and opaque, and diamond is hard and clear, for instance, because the two forms of carbon incorporate different lattices. Symmetry elements can be combined in groups, and 230 distinctive arrangements are possible. While the number of combinations of atoms and molecules is infinite, the number of their arrangements in three-dimensional space or form is limited to 230. Each of these arrangements is called a "space group," and all are listed and described in Volume A of the *International Tables for Crystallography* (see the section "Handbooks" below).

The most important results of a crystal structure determination are the x, y, z coordinates, together with unit cell parameters and symmetry information.[2] A structure determination (generally from single-crystal x-ray data) is well recognized as the highest material characterization level attainable.[3]

It is also important to note, especially with modern applications, the deviation from strict lattice order, structural defects, and order/disorder features are as much an area of study as are the ordered states.

HISTORY

Since early times, man has been intrigued by the perfect cubes of crystals in nature (e.g., minerals such a pyrite and quartz). In 1611, Johann Kepler published a small pamphlet on hexagonal snow suggesting that the regularity of crystal form is due to the regular geometrical arrangement of small building blocks.[4]

Crystallography grew out of a series of significant advances from a variety of disciplines and geographic areas. The interdisciplinary nature of the science emerged from the beginning in Germany (geological sciences, mineralogy), in Great Britain (physics), and the Netherlands (chemistry).[5] There followed a number of incremental advancements in physical, chemical, and mathematical sciences that formed the basis for understanding crystallographic structure of minerals and set the stage for the rapid change that was about to take place with the discovery of x-ray diffraction. A number of excellent works detail the history and development in each discipline and country: The works of José Lima-de-Faria,[6] Paul P. Ewald,[7] and D. McLachlan and J. P. Glusker[8] are among the best.

In 1877 the first journal devoted to crystallography was established, *Zeitschrift für Kristallographie und Mineralogie*. The articles published before the advent of x-ray crystallography in *Zeitschrift* reflected the growing understanding of crystal symmetry and morphology as well as the anisotropy of the related physical properties. Peter von Groth, in his seminal work *Physikalische Kristallographie* (1876), discussed the anisotropy of the physical properties of crystals in relation to their symmetry.[9] Walter Steurer notes that von Groth was already considering crystals to be composed of molecules at equilibrium positions on a regular network.[10] Most of the pioneering research in crystallography was conducted simultaneously and independently by physicists, chemists, mineralogists, and mathematicians around the turn of the twentieth century. The results were mainly published in journals of their respective communities, with only a smaller part appearing in the dedicated crystallography journals.

Modern crystallography was born in 1912 when Max von Laue and his group discovered that a beam of x-rays directed upon a crystal diffracted into a characteristic pattern, called the diffraction pattern. His experiments demonstrated both the wave nature of x-rays and the periodic arrangement of clusters of atoms in a crystal. Later, W. H. Bragg and his son, W. L. Bragg, were awarded the 1915 Nobel Prize in Chemistry for their development of crystal structure analysis using x-ray diffraction. To this day, a firm grasp of Bragg's law, the wavelength dependence of the diffraction, and the reciprocal lattice and its symmetry are central to understanding crystallography.[11] Further, no less than twenty-five additional Nobel Prizes have been awarded to scientists for their crystallographic-related work in the fields of physics, chemistry, physiology, and medicine,[12] including James Watson and Francis Crick, who deduced the double helix structure of DNA in 1953 in part from the results of x-ray diffraction analysis.

The continuing developments in x-ray diffraction, along with closely related advances in neutron and electron diffraction, have enabled scientists to discern the molecular patterns of nearly all solid substances. As the diffraction tools become more powerful with the availability of higher powered x-ray sources, such as those produced by synchrotrons, the brilliant x-rays allow researchers to collect their raw data much more quickly than when they had to use traditional sources. Synchrotrons were originally designed for use by high-energy physicists studying subatomic particles and cosmic phenomena. As S. J. L. Billenge notes, the availability of highly intense sources of x-rays and neutrons, and the ready availability of fast computing, allow extensive datasets (sometimes approaching gigabytes in size) to be analyzed and modeled.[13] These technological advances, coupled with the desire to study complex materials where diffuse scattering can hold the key to materials properties, are presenting new horizons for consideration.

Indeed, the science itself has outgrown the term "crystallography." Modern crystallography is clearly more than a description of crystals and their structures. Knowledge gained through the understanding of a substance's structure provides new insights into its properties, functions, and reactions.

INTERDISCIPLINARY NATURE

A special 2002 issue of *Zeitschrift für Kristallographie*[14] invited crystallographers from around the world to submit commentaries on the history, present state, and future of the science of crystallography. Andre Authier's contribution in this issue includes the following statement: "Crystallography is the science that studies the arrangements of atoms, ions, and molecules in solids and the properties that follow from these arrangements. . . . Crystallography is at the crossroads of mathematics, physics, chemistry, mineralogy, biochemistry and biology. Major developments of these sciences have depended, and will always depend on, the exact knowledge of these arrangements and of their properties."[15]

The fact that crystallography grew out of physics in England, out of chemistry in the Netherlands, and it was part of the geological sciences (mineralogy) in Germany attests to its interdisciplinary origin that continues to this day. The discovery of x-ray diffraction in 1912 set in motion a train of remarkable events that formed the modern science of crystallography. The profound impact of the crystallographic technique has been felt in physics, chemistry, mineralogy, metallurgy, biochemistry, and pharmacology and provides the essential structural impetus for developments in structural biology and molecular biophysics. The science of crystallography has also played a key role in the development of x-ray diffraction, electron diffraction, and neutron diffraction for the determination of the atomic structure of matter. Modern crystallography is an interdisciplinary branch of science taught in departments of physics, chemistry, geology, molecular biology, metallurgy, and material science at universities throughout the world.

H. Toyara[16] notes that there are generally two groups of crystallographers today. One is a minority group focused on developing instrumentation, methods, and algorithms for analyzing data and solving problems, including computer software. The second and majority group consists of those in the other scientific disciplines applying crystallographic techniques.

There is a symbiotic relationship between crystallographers and the scientists and engineers who employ crystallographic data in their disciplines. While crystallographic information provides new insights into the structure and properties of materials for solving the most important questions in these diverse areas of study, crystallographers are also dependent on the other disciplines for their own success and advancement. Computational software, visualization tools, and high performance computing, as well as large synchrotron radiation sources and other "big science" tools, are developed and employed to produce improved crystallographic techniques for the acquisition of new data. Even the methodology in which crystallographic data has been compiled and shared over the years has provided a model for data compilation used to map the human genome.

CRYSTALLOGRAPHIC INFORMATICS

The technology of computing renders the raw numeric diffraction data into patterns and structural bodies for observation and identification. This technology allows us to "see" molecular structure based on data from the waves of light, x-rays, electrons, neutrons, and protons.

The very nature of crystallography has led to a unique dependence on computers and information technology. Nearly all aspects of modern crystallography involve the use of computers, from data collections to structure solutions and refinement, to visualization, to complex databases.[17]

The field of crystallographic informatics requires a collaborative environment of computer scientists, chemists, biologists, and other specialties. Human-computer interaction as a field of research has led to immersive environments where researchers can walk through a crystal lattice or use tactile feedback to "feel" the surface of a crystal. New graphics systems are being developed that allow one to visualize and understand molecular structures and crystal packing in ways never before possible.

PROFESSIONAL SOCIETIES AND RESEARCH ORGANIZATIONS

The International Union of Crystallography (IUCr) promotes international cooperation in crystallography and contributes to all aspects of crystallographic research. The IUCr promotes international publication of crystallographic research, facilitates standardization of methods, units, nomenclatures, and symbols, and provides focus for the relations of crystallography to other scientific disciplines. The IUCr maintains a website (www.iucr.ac.uk) where directories of individuals involved in crystallographic research, links to related societies, and a wealth of additional information can be found. In addition to the IUCr, many national and local organizations exist to promote crystallographic research as well as divisions within other professional societies in chemistry, biology, physics, and materials sciences. D. Schwarzenbach notes, "Interdisciplinarity is still something that politicians and funding agencies want to happen. One should make clear that the IUCr, (is) the only truly interdisciplinary organization in the exact sciences."[18]

Several research institutions around the world dedicate a sizeable portion of their research activities to acquiring, producing, and standardizing crystallographic data. Among the most active are the U.S. National Institute of Standards and Technology (NIST), the International Centre for Diffraction Data (ICDD), and Fachinformationzentrum (FIZ) Karlsruhe. These three organizations are also responsible for hosting important crystallographic databases that will be listed later in the chapter.

STRUCTURE OF THE LITERATURE

The published literature in crystallography centers around the announcement of structure determinations reported in journal articles, conference papers, and reports. Before the advent of computerization, and even for some time afterwards, the reported data (the substance's molecular coordinates) were extracted and republished in tabular format in handbooks and other multivolume serial publications such as *Strukture Berichte* as far back at the late 1800s.

Since the coordinate data is primarily numeric and systematic in nature, computerization of crystallographic information was a natural evolution. In fact, crystallography was one of the first scientific disciplines to computerize and one of the first to offer widespread access to its numerical databases. Over the past forty years, virtually all identified structure determinations have been archived in databases, which allow electronic access and provide comprehensive coverage of the literature.

The remainder of this chapter will focus on the important print and electronic resources for acquiring and interpreting crystallographic information. The reader will be presented with a list of basic scientific resources that describe the importance of crystallographic data from the point of view of various disciplines. The primary print handbooks, tables, and compilations will be identified in later sections. Accessing the journal literature will be addressed under "Journals" and "Abstracting and Indexing Services." Finally, the important databases that contain almost all the existing crystallographic data will be identified. As with any modern scientific discipline, there has been a continual evolution toward the electronic access and delivery of published information on the Internet. Important crystallographic websites will also be identified.

The structure of the published literature, both online and in print, are generally covered in these types of publications:

general overviews
history
treatise/monographs/textbooks
journal articles
abstracting and indexing sources
handbooks/manuals
electronic databases
Internet resources

Many of the print and electronic resources reporting crystallographic structural information focus on one or more of the following physical categories:

elements
minerals
inorganic substances
organic substances
biological and/or macromolecules
metals

Additionally, information on the laboratory techniques and tools used to collect and analyze crystallographic data can be generally grouped into these categories:

methodology /techniques
instrumentation
laboratory devices
computational services

GENERAL OVERVIEWS AND HISTORICAL WORKS

For the nonscientist interested in understanding the basics of crystal structure and its importance in any number of scientific disciplines, the best nontechnical descriptions will be found in general encyclopedias. The entries under "crystallography" in *Encyclopedia Britannica,* the *McGraw-Hill Encyclopedia of Science and Technology,* and even the upstart *Wikipedia.org* provide excellent overviews of the subject.

For those with some existing knowledge of the scientific mathematics of physics and chemistry who wish to understand a little more about crystallography from an advanced level, K. Ann Kerr's chapter in *The Encyclopedia of Physical Science and Technology,*[19] along with W. B. Pearson and C. Cheih's contribution to *Encyclopedia of Applied Physics,*[20] are good starting points for further study.

For the librarian or information specialist, the crystallographic literature (both published and electronic) has been studied in just a few articles and book chapters. Donald T. Hawkins described the interdisciplinary nature of the literature in detail in 1980 with a bibliometric and citation analysis.[21] Gregory K. Youngen updated the work in 2000 and included many of the newer electronic resources in the field.[22] Mackay also wrote a noteworthy analysis of the field in Shaw's *Use of Physics Literature.*[23] An excellent, although somewhat dated at this time, overview of the major electronic databases in crystallography was published in 1987 by the IUCr.[24] A special 1996 issue of the *Journal of Research of the National Institute of Standards and Technology*[25] also provides a state-of-the-art review of the issues associated with the existing crystallographic databases at the time of writing.

The history of the scientific discoveries in the field of crystallography, as well as its emergence as a multidisciplinary field of study, are well documented in a number of excellent sources published over the past fifty years. John G. Burke[26] looks at the historical development of Crystallography as a science, and Lima-de-Faria's *Historical Atlas of Crystallography*[27] documents the major milestones achieved by scientists and researchers in the field. D. McLachlan and J. P. Gusker[28] focus on the significant North American contributions in the field. The developments of x-ray and electron diffraction techniques in crystallography are addressed by Paul P. Ewald[29] and P. Goodman,[30] respectively. Harmke Kamminga's[31] description of the founding and development of the IUCr is also of historical significance in the field.

INTRODUCTORY TEXTS

Every discipline has its own emphasis in the study and use of crystallographic data. The titles listed in this section are representative of introductory textbooks in a number of fields focusing on the study of crystallography and the utilization of crystallographic techniques.

CRYSTAL STRUCTURE AND DIFFRACTION TECHNIQUES

The scientific basis of crystal patterns and structures are addressed in two classic texts by Noel F. Kennon[32] and Arthur P. Cracknell.[33] The physical properties of crystals and lattices are also covered by J. F. Nye.[34] Methods and tools used to determine crystal structure, including x-ray and electron diffraction, electron microscopy, and the modern high intensity radiation sources are covered by a large number of works. Among the introductory texts that may be of interest to those seeking an overview of the study of crystallography are those by Walter Borchardt-Ott,[35] Duncan McKie,[36] and Jean-Jacques Rosseau.[37] Diffraction techniques are covered by Bernard D. Cullity and S. R. Stock,[38] Christopher Hammond,[39] and Michael M. Woolfson.[40]

MATHEMATICS/COMPUTER SCIENCE

The basis for understanding crystal structure and visually representing structure from diffraction patterns requires a strong mathematical foundation. The *International Tables for Crystallography* (Vol. A) provides an overview of the basic mathematical concepts in crystallography. Monte B. Boisen's[41] introductory text in mathematical crystallography is another good source. Perhaps the most complex stage of diffraction and crystallography occurs not with the actual experiment, but with the reconstruction of the diffraction patterns for analysis. After the sample material has diffracted the x-rays, the reconstruction process involves elaborate mathematical manipulations based on the scattered radiation patterns. Adam Morwiec[42] and Rob Phillips[43] have recent books on computational crystallography and modeling.

MINERALOGY/GEOSCIENCES

The field of mineralogy owned crystallography until physics got involved with the advent of x-ray diffraction in 1912. crystallography and mineralogy were closely tied in late nineteenth- and early twentieth-century German research and publication. The journal *Zeitschrift für Mineralogie und Kristallographie* established in 1877 was the leading publication in the field. Today, geoscientists employ crystallographic methods to contribute to the understanding of the structure of the earth's crust and upper mantle, the moon and meteorites, as well as geologic time-dependent reactions. Lima-de-Faria's[44] book on structural mineralogy and Eric J. W. Whittaker's[45] introductory work on crystallography for earth science students are excellent sources.

PHYSICS

The relationship between physics and crystallography is particularly close. In part, this is due to the physical techniques employed: diffraction, topography, and spectroscopy. But to a larger extent, the close relationship is due to the profound impact crystallography has had on our understanding of the nature and structure of matter.[46] The goal in solid state physics is to predict the structure and properties of materials. Crystallography makes important contributions toward this goal, such as providing crystal structure and data, like orbital order, that are used to develop and test new theoretical models. Charles Kittel's[47] introductory textbook on solid state physics is required reading in most undergraduate and graduate studies. Works by Ajit Ram Verma[48] and H. M. Rosenberg[49] are also important contributions in solid state physics and crystallography.

CHEMISTRY

From a chemist's point of view, one of the most fundamental pieces of information about a chemical compound is the way its atoms are arranged in space.[50] The importance of x-ray structure determination in molecular chemistry is demonstrated by the fact that it became the main method for the analysis of the constitution of substances from small molecules up to polymers and proteins. Tony Stankus notes, "Modern biochemistry owes a debt to inorganic chemists' preoccupation with structural matters, particularly the structure of crystals. Inorganic chemists long ago learned from physicists and mineralogists the power of x-rays to indicate structure, and have passed this on to chemists working with proteins and nucleic acids. Many complex biochemicals, much like coordination compounds, can be crystallized for much more rapid analysis using x-rays than would be possible using 'wet' chemical tests. The various formulas for converting patterns on exposed x-ray films into coordinates for three-dimensional views were developed by inorganic crystallographers."[51] Donald F. Bloss[52] and J. P. Glusker[53] provide overviews of crystallography that focus on chemical aspects of molecular structure. Additionally, Collings' introduction to liquid crystals is noteworthy. [54]

BIOLOGY/MEDICINE

In biology, the structural solution of the DNA double helix ushered in rapid developments in the field of molecular biology. Crystallographic methods allow the determination of complicated three-dimensional structures of proteins consisting of thousands of atoms in such detail that determinations of their chemical and biological functions became possible. All biological processes are regulated and carried out by nucleic acids (DNA) and proteins. These processes can only be understood if the spatial structures of the complicated macromolecules—and in particular, the geometry of their active centers—are known in atomic detail. Since it is possible to crystallize nucleic acids, proteins, and even intact viruses, they are accessible to x-ray structure analysis; therefore crystallography is key to determining this information. X-ray crystallography is often used to determine how drugs, such as anti-cancer medications, can be improved to better influence their protein targets. M. Vijayan notes, "The most promising hunting grounds for crystallography are biology and materials science, in that order."[55] David M. Blow's *Outline of Crystallography for Biologists*[56] is an essential work in the field. Alexander McPherson[57] and Gale Rhodes[58] provide introductory works on the crystallographic study of macromolecules, while Jan Drenth[59] addresses protein x-ray crystallography.

ACCESSING THE PRIMARY LITERATURE

Journals

As mentioned previously, reports and announcements of new structure determinations appear first in journal articles, technical reports, or conference proceedings. Almost all significant findings eventually appear in the journal literature. There are approximately sixty-five primary journals publishing crystallographic data, originally identified by Hawkins[60] in 1980, and updated by Youngen[61] twenty years later. The core journal list includes titles important to the study of crystallography as well as other titles in chemistry, physics, biology, and the materials sciences where crystallographic data is an important part of the ongoing research. The crystallographic data published in journal articles is often simultaneously provided to the database producers, so the information is available in electronic format often before it appears in print. Some of the data will also eventually appear in the handbooks, tables, and manuals in print format.

The relative importance of individual journals publishing crystallographic information can be measured by the number of citations the articles receive from other crystallographic publications. The top ten journals publishing crystallographic articles by impact factor, according to the Institute for Scientific Information in 2002, are listed below.[62]

1. *Journal of Crystal Growth*
2. *Journal of Applied Crystallography*
3. *Acta Crystallographica A*
4. *Acta Crystallographica B*
5. *Acta Crystallographica D*
6. *Polyhedron*
7. *Acta Crystallographica C*
8. *Molecular Crystals and Liquid Crystals*
9. *Liquid Crystals*
10. *Zeitschrift für Kristallographie*

Abstracting and Indexing Services

The two primary sources for accessing the crystallographic journal literature are *Chemical Abstracts* and *Inspec*. Both are computer-based search services that provide up-to-date and historical access to journal articles, conference papers, and technical reports in chemistry and physics, respectively. While there is some overlap in the coverage of these two enormous databases, there are distinctions in the scope, breadth, and depth of the literature they index. The differences can also be seen in the way they subdivide the subject area of crystallography.

Chemical Abstracts' subject division on crystallography (Section 75) generally divides the discipline by material type and structure:

CA Section 75—Crystallization and Crystal Structure Reviews

1. Crystallization
   Methods and theory
   Nucleation
   Growth (including twinning)
   Effect of impurities
2. Order-disorder and dislocations
3. Phase transformation of crystals
4. Physical properties of crystals
5. Crystal structure determination
   Methods and theory - elements, metals
   Inorganic compounds
   Organic compounds
   Mesomorphic (liquid crystalline) phases
   Liquids
   Gases

On the other hand, *Inspec* tends to focus its subject categorization on process rather than material type:

Section 6100: Structure of liquids and solids; crystallography
6110 X-ray determination of structures
6112 Neutron determination of structures
6114 Electron determination of structures
6116 Other determination of structures
6120 Classical, semiclassical, and quantum theories of liquid structure
6125 Studies of specific liquid structures
6130 Liquid crystals
6140 Amorphous

Chemical Abstracts is perhaps the best single source for access to all areas of crystallographic research due to its broad coverage of the chemical literature. Most of the journals likely to publish crystallographic data will at least be selectively indexed by *Chemical Abstracts*. *Inspec* will be of interest to physicists needing data on inorganic compounds, especially where materials for electronic applications are being studied. *Inspec* would also provide excellent coverage of the engineering side of instrumentation and devices being used and developed for the extraction of crystallographic properties.

There are also several other abstracting and indexing services for specific areas of the literature. Some of these titles predate both *Chemical Abstracts* and *Inspec* and must be relied upon for comprehensive coverage of the international literature and/or material dating back to the beginnings of the study of crystallography.

1. *Metals Abstracts.* ASM International, 1968–. (Available electronically as METADEX). Section Heading 12: Crystal structure.
2. *Minerals Abstracts.* The Mineralogical Society. 1920–. (Available online as MINABS; www.minabs.com/).
3. *Zentralblatt fuer Mineralogie.* Teil 1, 1807–. Kristallographie und Mineralogie.
4. *Bulletin Signaletique.* Centre National de la Recherche Scientifique, 1969–. Section 161. Cristallographie.

Handbooks and Manuals

There have been many crystallographic reference works published since the beginning of the twentieth century. Many of these handbooks and manuals collected and compiled the existing crystallographic structural data of the time and published it in single or multivolume serial format. Other manuals provide detailed information on the crystallographic techniques of the day, along with the data compiled from the various collection methods. Most of the information published in these titles has been subsumed by the databases that now provide the data electronically. Youngen compiled a cross-reference listing of the data that shows in which databases that information, once published in print, presently resides. This section will only focus on those print titles with unique and lasting value to the crystallographer that are still in some process of being updated.

The single most important print resource in the crystallography reference collection is the International Union of Crystallography's *International Tables for Crystallography*.[63] This multivolume work, commonly referred to as the "crystallographer's bible," supplies essential information on the basics of crystal structure determination and symmetry, along with the mathematical and physical science foundations for understanding the crystallographic process. It also includes a teaching volume as an introduction to using the tables.

The *CRC Handbook of Chemistry and Physics* is another essential resource, available electronically and in print, that provides basic crystallographic structure information on the elements, some inorganic compounds, magnetic materials, minerals, and semi- and superconductors.

The long-published series, *Landolt-Bornstein: Numerical Data and Functional Relationships in Science and Technology*, has a collection of volumes (Group III) dedicated to crystal and solid state physics. *Landolt-Bornstein* includes historical and up-to-date information on structural data of crystals and special volumes on organic, inorganic, and intermetallic compounds. Most of the data reported in *Landolt-Bornstein* is also available in the *Inorganic Crystal Structure Database* ([ICSD], see "Database" section).

The *Metals Handbook*, (10th ed., 1991) is an encyclopedic handbook containing crystal structure information on specific metals and alloys. It also provides significant coverage of the basics of crystallography, including diffraction methods, microscopy, and other materials science applications related to metals and metallography.

A work originating from the geology community, *Mineral Physics and Crystallography: A Handbook of Physical Constants* (American Geophysical Union, 1995), contains selected critical data on the characterizations and crystallographic properties of over 300 minerals. It is the successor to the core reference title, *Handbook of Physical Constants* (Geological Society of America, 1942 and 1966).

Structure Reports (International Union of Crystallography, 1913–1943) is the most comprehensive print listing of the crystallographic data available. While most of its contents are available electronically through a number of databases, the longevity (since 1913) and scope (including organic and inorganic compounds, but excluding proteins) of the work make it notable for inclusion. Originally published in German as *Strukturebericht*, nearly

200 volumes of tabulated data provide critically reviewed information on crystal structures including formulas, unit cells, and space group data, details of analysis, atomic positions, and sources for the data reported.

Databases

Since their inception, crystallographic databases have had the common aim of recording not only the relevant bibliographic and chemical information needed for searching and for access to the original literature, but also the often extensive primary numerical results of the experimental data. There are five major crystallographic databases continuously maintained and updated: *Cambridge Structural Database, Inorganic Crystal Structure Database, Protein Data Bank, Nucleic Acids Database,* and *Powder Diffraction File.*[64] Some of these databases are freely accessible, but others require a subscription. It is also important to remember that information on some structures obtained by private research organizations may be proprietary, especially medicinally relevant proteins or other commercially viable products. Information on these structures would not be deposited in public crystallographic databases and might therefore be inaccessible.

In addition to the major crystallographic databases, several recent databases and new applications are listed in this section. Many of these are web based and offer enhanced search and display capabilities. Additional information on the databases listed here, as well as an overview of the current state of crystallographic databases in general, can be found in Allen[65] and Youngen.[66]

The *Cambridge Structural Database* (CSD) produced by the Cambridge Crystallographic Data Center ([CCDC], www.ccdc.cam.ac.uk/products/csd/), contains information on over 335,000 experimentally determined crystal structures of organic and organometallic compounds, including drugs, natural products, and chemicals compiled since 1935. All of these crystal structures have been analyzed using x-ray or neutron diffraction techniques. Each crystallographic entry in the CSD provides bibliographic information, chemical connectivity, and numeric data. The CCDC has developed graphical search, retrieval, and data visualization software for accessing the CSD.

The Inorganic Crystal Structure Database (ICSD) is produced by the Gmelin-Institute for Inorganic Studies, FIZ Karlsruhe (www.fiz-informationsdienste.de/en/DB/icsd/). ICSD is a comprehensive compilation of crystal structure data of inorganic compounds. All information has been obtained from the original sources and checked to assure high quality. The literature is covered back to 1915. Earlier papers were located by searching *Strukturbericht, Structure Reports, Crystal Data,* and *Landolt-Bornstein.* The database is now updated by direct scanning of major journals. Currently the database contains over 86,000 entries and is updated semiannually, and approximately 2,500 new entries are added each year.

The *Nucleic Acid Database Project* ([NDB], ndbserver.rutgers.edu/NDB/), provided by Rutgers University, contains three-dimensional structural information on RNA and DNA oligonucleotides that have been obtained from x-ray crystallographic experiments. The NDB allows retrieval of coordinates and provides information about the conditions used to derive the coordinates and the structural information that could be derived from the coordinates.

The *Powder Diffraction File* (PDF), produced by the Joint Committee on Powder Diffraction Standards and the International Center for Diffraction Data (www.icdd.com/), is the most comprehensive database for single-phase x-ray powder diffraction patterns. The entire database consists of nearly 500,000 material datasets and is updated yearly. The primary use of the PDF is to identify "fingerprints" of unknown materials by matching the spacings of the unknown material's diffraction patterns with the spacings of known substances.

The *Protein Data Bank* (PDB) provided by the U.S. Department of Energy, Brookhaven National Laboratory (www.rcsb.org), is an electronic archive of experimentally determined three-dimensional structures of proteins, nucleic acids, and other biological macromolecules. The database contains atomic coordinates, bibliographic citations, primary and secondary structure information, as well as crystallographic structure factors and nuclear magnetic resonance (NMR) experimental data. The PDB primarily contains data from diffraction and NMR studies of proteins, nucleic acids, and viruses. It is the single global archive of such data, and it is thus of enormous value to many scientific and industrial communities.

Other Databases and Internet Resources

The IUCr maintains an up-to-date web page for many crystallographic databases, teaching tools, and other information sources (journals.iucr.org/cww-top/crystal.index.html).

The *Biological Macromolecule Crystallization Database* (BMCD), produced by NIST (www.cstl.nist.gov/biotech/carb/gilliland_group/database/database.html), contains crystal data and the crystallization conditions compiled from the published literature. The current version of the BMCD includes crystallographic data from biological macromolecules for which diffraction-quality crystals have been obtained. These include proteins, protein-protein complexes, nucleic acid, nucleic acid-nucleic acid complexes, protein-nucleic acid complexes, and viruses. In addition to including crystallization data reported in the literature, the BMCD contains the *NASA Protein Crystal Growth Archive*, which includes the crystallization data generated from studies carried out in a microgravity environment supported by NASA. Data from other crystallization experiments carried out under microgravity sponsored by other international space agencies are also included.

Crystal Lattice Structures, produced by the U.S. Naval Research Laboratory (cst-www.nrl.navy.mil/lattice/) is a web-based data file offering a concise index of common crystal lattice structures. A graphical representation as well as useful information about the lattices can be obtained by clicking on the available structure diagrams.

The *Electron Diffraction Database*, produced in cooperation with NIST and Sandia National Laboratory (www.nist.gov/srd/nist15.htm), contains crystallographic and chemical information on over 87,200 crystalline materials—a large fraction of which are unique phases—for application to electron diffraction. Each entry contains space group data, unit cell data, chemical formula and name, and literature references. Designed for phase characterization obtained by electron diffraction methods, this database and associated software permit highly selective identification procedures for microscopic and macroscopic crystalline materials. The database contains crystallographic information on a wide variety of materials including minerals, metals, intermetallics, and general inorganic compounds.

CONCLUSION

The multidisciplinary role of crystallography in physics, chemistry, geology, and biology has been established. Crystallography provides profound insights into the structure of solid matter, and the modern databases are powerful and cost-effective tools for solving materials identification problems. The developments in this field have provided the ability to examine three-dimensional shapes of molecules and their mutual arrangements in addition to the intra- and intermolecular interactions and relationships between the structure and properties of chemical compounds in the crystalline state. Recent progress in understanding chemical bonds, life processes, and the function of drugs, as well as designing new materials, would not be possible without the contributions of crystallography.

NOTES

1. Alan L. Mackay, "Crystallography," in *Information Sources in Physics*, ed. Dennis Shaw (Boston: Butterworths, 1985), 133–45.

2. Fran H. Allen, "The Development, Status and Scientific Impact of Crystallographic Databases," *Acta Crystallographica A*, A54 (1998): 759–71.

3. Armel Le Bail, "Unknowns in Chemical Company's Catalogs," in 2nd *International Electronic Conference on Synthetic Organic Chemistry* (ECSOC-2), September 1–30, 1998, at pages.unibas.ch/mdpi/ecsoc-2old.htm (accessed October 18, 2005).

4. Johannes Kepler, *The Six-Cornered Snowflake*, trans. Colin Hardie (Oxford: Clarendon Press, 1966).

5. S. van Smaalen, "Crystallography through Time within the Sciences," *Zeitschrift für Kristallographie* 217, no. 7/8 (2002): 376–77.

6. José Lima-de-Faria, *Historical Atlas of Crystallography* (Dordrecht: Kluwer Academic Publishers, 1990).

7. Paul P. Ewald, ed., *Fifty Years of X-ray Diffraction* (Utrecht: N.V.A. Ossthoek, 1962).

8. D. McLachlan and J. P. Glusker, eds., *Crystallography in North America* (New York: American Crystallographic Association, 1983).

9. Peter von Groth, *Physikalische Kristallographie und Einleitung in die Krystallographische Kenntniss der Wichtigeren Substanzen* (Leipzig: Engelmann, 1876).

10. Walter Steurer, "Crystallography and Crystallographers," *Zeitschrift für Kristallographie* 217, no. 7/8 (2002): 267.

11. Frank C. Phillips, *An Introduction to Crystallography*, 4th ed. (New York: Wiley, 1972).

12. British Crystallographic Association, "Nobel Prize Winners Associated with Crystallography," January 12, 2002, at bca.cryst.bbk.ac.uk/BCA/Cnews/1997/Sep97/Nobels.html (accessed November 2005).

13. S. J. L. Billenge, "Complex Materials: Beyond Crystallography," *Zeitschrift für Kristallographie* 217, no. 7/8 (2002): 282.

14. *Zeitschrift für Kristallographie* 217, no. 7/8 (2002).

15. Andre Authier, "What is Crystallography: A Personal Opinion," *Zeitschrift für Kristallographie* 217, no. 7/8 (2002): 276–77.

16. H. Toyara, "Personal Reflections," *Zeitschrift für Kristallographie* 217, no. 7/8 (2002): 375.

17. John C. Huffman, "Crystallographic Informatics," *Zeitschrift für Kristallographie* 217, no. 7/8 (2002): 320–21.

18. D. Schwarzenbach, "What is Crystallography?" *Zeitschrift für Kristallographie* 217, no. 7/8 (2002): 366.

19. K. Ann Kerr, *Crystallography*, vol. 4 of *The Encyclopedia of Physical Science and Technology*, ed. Robert A. Meyers (San Diego: Academic Press, 1992): 757–95.

20. W. B. Pearson and C. Cheih, *Crystallography*, vol. 4 of *Encyclopedia of Applied Physics*, ed. George Trigg (New York: VCH, 1992): 385–408.

21. Donald T. Hawkins, "Crystallographic Literature: A Bibliometric and Citation Analysis," *Acta Crystallographica A*, A36 (1980): 475–82.

22. Gregory K. Youngen, "A Guide to Information Resources in Crystallography," *Science and Technology Libraries* 19, no. 1 (2000): 49–78.

23. Mackay, "Crystallography," 133–45.

24. F. H. Allen, ed., *International Union of Crystallography, Data Commission, Crystallographic Databases* (Bonn: IUCr, 1987).

25. *Journal of Research of the National Institute of Standards and Technology* 101, no. 3 (1996): 205–380.

26. John G. Burke, *Origins of the Science of Crystals* (Berkeley: University of California Press, 1966).

27. Lima-de-Faria, *Historical Atlas of Crystallography*.

28. McLachlan and Glusker, eds., *Crystallography in North America*.

29. Ewald, ed., *Fifty Years of X-ray Diffraction*.

30. P. Goodman, ed., *Fifty Years of Electron Diffraction* (Dordrecht: D. Reidel Publishing Company, 1981).

31. Harmke Kamminga, "The International Union of Crystallography: Its Formation and Early Development," *Acta Crystallographica*, A45 (1989): 581–601.

32. Noel F. Kennon, *Patterns in Crystals* (Chichester: Wiley, 1978).

33. Arthur P. Cracknell, *Crystals and Their Structures* (Oxford, New York: Pergamon Press, 1969).

34. J. F. Nye, *Physical Properties of Crystals: Their Representation by Tensors and Matrices* (New York: Clarendon Press, 1984).

35. Walter Borchardt-Ott, *Crystallography*, 2nd ed. (New York: Springer-Verlag, 1995).

36. Duncan McKie, *Essentials of Crystallography* (Oxford: Blackwell Scientific Publications, 1986).

37. Jean-Jacques Rousseau, *Basic Crystallography* (New York: Wiley, 1998).

38. Bernard D. Cullity and S. R. Stock., *Elements of X-Ray Diffraction*, 3rd ed. (New York: Prentice-Hall, 2001).

39. Christopher Hammond, *The Basics of Crystallography and Diffraction* (Oxford: Oxford University Press, 1997).

40. Michael M. Woolfson, *An Introduction to X-ray Crystallography*, 2nd ed. (New York: Cambridge University Press, 1997).

41. Monte B. Boisen, *Mathematical Crystallography: An Introduction to the Mathematical Foundations of Crystallography* (Washington, DC: Mineralogical Society of America, 1985).

42. Adam Morawiec, *Orientations and Rotations: Computations in Crystallographic Textures* (New York: Springer, 2004).

43. Rob Phillips, *Crystals, Defects and Microstructures: Modeling Across Scales* (Cambridge: Cambridge University Press, 2001).

44. José Lima-de-Faria, *Structural Mineralogy: An Introduction* (Dordrecht: Kluwer Academic Publishers, 1994).

45. Eric J. W. Whittaker, *Crystallography: An Introduction for Earth Science and Other Solid State Students* (New York: Pergamon, 1981).

46. Von Smaalen, "Crystallography through Time within the Sciences," 376–77.

47. Charles Kittel, *Introduction to Solid State Physics*, 8th ed. (New York: Wiley, 2005).

48. Ajit Ram Verma, *Crystallography for Solid State Physics* (New York: Wiley, 1982).

49. H. M. Rosenberg, *The Solid State: An Introduction to the Physics of Crystals for Students of Physics, Materials Science, and Engineering*, 3rd ed. (Oxford, New York: Oxford University Press, 1988).

50. Michael O'Keeffe and Bruce G. Hyde, *Crystal Structures: I. Patterns and Symmetry* (Washington, DC: Mineralogical Society of America, 1996).

51. Tony Stankus, *Making Sense of Journals in the Physical Sciences* (New York: Haworth Press, 1992), 42.

52. Donald F. Bloss, *Crystallography and Crystal Chemistry: An Introduction* (Washington, DC: Mineralogical Society of America, 1994).

53. J. P. Glusker, ed., *Structural Crystallography in Chemistry and Biology* (Stroudsburg, PA: Hutchinson, 1981).

54. Peter J. Collings, *Introduction to Liquid Crystals: Chemistry and Physics* (London: Taylor & Francis, 1997).

55. M. Vijayan, "Personal Reflections," *Zeitschrift für Kristallographie* 217, no. 7/8 (2002): 378.

56. David M. Blow, *Outline of Crystallography for Biologists* (Oxford: Oxford University Press, 2002).

57. Alexander McPherson, *Introduction to Macromolecular Crystallography* (New York: Wiley, 2002).

58. Gale Rhodes, *Crystallography Made Crystal Clear: A Guide for Users of Macromolecular Models,* 2nd ed. (New York: Academic Press, 1999).

59. Jan Drenth, *Principles of Protein X-ray Crystallography* (New York: Springer, 1999).

60. Donald T. Hawkins, "Crystallographic Literature: A Bibliometric and Citation Analysis," *Acta Crystallographica A*, A36 (1980): 475–82.

61. Gregory K. Youngen, "A Guide to Information Resources in Crystallography," *Science and Technology Libraries* 19, no. 1 (2000): 49–78.

62. Institute for Scientific Information Journal Citation Reports, 2002.

63. International Union for Crystallography, *International Tables for Crystallography.* Published by Dordrecht. Volumes include the following: *Vol. A, Space-group Symmetry* (1983); *Vol. A1, Symmetry Relations between Space Groups* (2004); *Vol. B, Reciprocal Space* (1993); *Vol. C, Mathematical, Physical, and Chemical Tables* (1992); *Vol. D, Physical Properties of Crystals* (2003); *Vol. E, Subperiodic Groups* (2002); and *Vol. F, Crystallography of Biological Macromolecules* (2001).

64. Gregory K. Youngen, *Crystallography and Crystallographic Information* at www.library.uiuc.edu/phx/crystal/crystalrev.html (accessed August 1, 2006).

65. Allen, "The Development, Status and Scientific Impact of Crystallographic Databases," 759–71.

66. Youngen, "A Guide to Information Resources in Crystallography," 49–78.

3

Quaternary Research

Lura Joseph

WHAT IS QUATERNARY RESEARCH?[1]

Quaternary research (QR) is the study of the Quaternary, the geologic period of time that spans approximately the last two million years of the Earth's geologic history.[2] The Quaternary geologic time period includes the Pleistocene (approximately two million years to ten thousand years ago), sometimes known as the Ice Age, and the Holocene (approximately ten thousand years ago to the present), the geologic epoch in which we live. Scientists currently disagree regarding the exact boundaries and dates for the Quaternary and whether to retain it as a formal chronostratigraphic unit.[3] In fact, the most recent International Commission on stratigraphy has removed the term "Quaternary" from the International Geologic Time Scale and included that period of time in the Neogene period.[4]

The Quaternary has been a time of frequent, extreme, and often abrupt climate and environmental changes, during which continental and mountain glaciers advanced and retreated.[5] These climate and environmental changes were accompanied by global changes in floral and faunal communities, including extinctions of megafauna and the evolution and dispersal of humans. The climate of the Earth currently appears to be warming, which may portend significant and rapid environmental changes that could challenge modern civilization. Currently, a major goal of QR is to document past climate patterns at various time scales in order to understand current trends and to predict future climate patterns and environmental effects.

The study of the Quaternary time period is extremely interdisciplinary.[6] Those studying the Quaternary include specialists in the following disciplines: anthropology/archaeology, biology, botany, climatology, ecology, entomology, geochronology, geography, geology, geomorphology, geophysics, glaciology, hydrogeology, isotope geochemistry, limnology, oceanology, molecular genetics, paleoceanography, paleoecology, paleontology, palynology, planetary geology, soil science/pedology, structural geology/neotectonics, volcanology, and zoology. Researchers study ice cores; ocean sediments; ocean circulation; lake sediments; fossils and modern animals and plants including vertebrates, invertebrates, insects, and pollen; cycles of the earth/sun; atmosphere; and others. Of importance are atmospheric, ocean, and terrestrial interactions and the building of testable computer models.

HISTORY AND DEVELOPMENT OF QUATERNARY RESEARCH

Quaternary geology has beginnings as a branch of historical geology.[7] During the time that geology was beginning as a science, Giovanni Arduino (1713–1795) proposed a four-fold geochronologic division from earliest to latest: Primary, Secondary, Tertiary, and Quaternary.[8] The use of the first two terms has been discontinued, while the last two continue. In 1829, Jules Desnoyers proposed the term Quaternary for certain outcrops in France, being convinced that they were younger than Tertiary rocks. In the following decade, the Quaternary was further subdivided into the Pleistocene and Holocene series.

In the early nineteenth century, research included glacial and interglacial studies, along with related studies of flora, fauna, spores, and pollen. By the middle of the nineteenth century, geologists recognized that large-scale changes had occurred in landscape and environment during the Ice Age.[9] In Russia, regular studies of the Quaternary strata began after the establishment of the Geological Committee in 1882.[10] The twentieth century saw an increase of interest in the relationship between Quaternary stratigraphy and topographic features; human Paleolithic distribution related to stratigraphy; neotectonics and seismotectonics; pedology (soils); and correlation of marine and continental deposits. During the last thirty years, data from deep sea drilling have indicated that climate cooling started about twenty-five million years ago. In recent years, climate change dynamics have become the focus of most QR.

In 1928, the International Union for Quaternary Research (INQUA) was founded by a group of scientists who were conducting interdisciplinary research into environmental changes that occurred during the glacial ages.[11]

Previously, the Russians had founded the International Association for Studying the Quaternary Period of Europe, and the Commission for Studying the Quaternary Period was established by the Russian Academy of Sciences in 1927. INQUA began holding international congresses in 1928. Congresses are held every four or five years, although there was a gap in the 1940s. Attendance may reach one thousand participants. There are more than thirty-five member countries worldwide.

There are several defining programs and events in the history of QR. One such event was the initiation of the Deep Sea Drilling Program. In 1964, four major oceanographic organizations formed the Joint Oceanographic Institutions for Deep Earth Sampling, and a fifth institution joined in 1968. After preliminary drilling in 1965, the Deep Sea Drilling Project began in 1968.[12] The sediment from the cores recovered by this project provides solid data that can be used in long-term climate analysis, and subsequently, climate change research became an important and continuing part of QR. The Ocean Drilling Program continues to this day.

Other programs with major implications for QR are the ice drilling projects in the Arctic and Antarctic regions. Deep-ice-core drilling projects in both regions took place from the early 1960s to the 1980s. Two deep-ice-core projects drilled deeper than three kilometers in Greenland between 1989 and 1993 and provided important data related to climate change over the past 250,000 years. The data provided unequivocal evidence that "The Earth has experienced large, rapid, regional to global climate oscillations through most of the last 110,000 years on a scale that human agriculture and industrial activities have not yet faced."[13] Data from these two cores are still being analyzed and used by researchers, and new drilling has continued in the Arctic and Antarctic regions. Recovery of a new ice core from Dome C, Antarctica, has provided a climate record for the past 740,000 years.[14] The precision and detail of the deep-sea core and deep-ice-core data promoted a variety of research devoted to the study of climate change; the research incorporated and unified diverse factors that serve as climate proxies.

The 1965 INQUA meeting in Denver, Colorado was a defining event for the United States.[15] It was after the Denver meeting that QR matured in America. In addition to INQUA, there are a number of related societies and associations that have helped to maintain and foster QR as a distinct area of science.[16] Besides the Russian association and commission, it appears that INQUA remained the only formal organization for QR until the Germans established Deutsche Quartärvereinigung in 1951. The French and the British established Quaternary associations in the 1960s, Association Française pour l'Etude du Quaternaire and Quaternary Research Association, respectively. Five Quaternary associations were formed during the 1970s; three began in the 1980s, and several more were started in the 1990s.

The proliferation of professional publications also illustrates the growth of QR. The first specialized journal devoted to QR was likely *Eiszeitalter und Gegenwart: Jahrbuch der Deutschen Quartärvereinigung*, which began publication in 1951. Most of the major QR journals began publication in the 1970s and 1980s.

The field of QR is sustained through regular international, national, and local meetings; field trips; working groups and commissions; publications including journals, newsletters, and monographs and monographic series; and networking, electronic discussion lists, and various sources of funding.

STRUCTURE AND UNIQUE
CHARACTERISTICS OF THE LITERATURE

Significant Primary Resources

QR information is disseminated via a number of resources including journals, conference proceedings, monographic series and books, government documents, field trip guide books, and reports of working groups. Researchers are able to submit their results to a number of journals devoted primarily to QR.[17] In addition, articles related to QR can be found in a number of other subject-specific journals and general geology journals.

Reference Resources

Handbooks

Many Quaternary researchers make use of handbooks for their specialty and also for related areas. For example, a researcher whose specialty is the study of fossil beetles will often consult handbooks to aid in identification of specimens. Since beetles adjusted to environmental change during the Quaternary primarily by moving to different latitudes and elevations rather than by evolving, fossil beetles are compared to modern specimens to help interpret climate change. Examples of handbooks that might be used are *The Ground-Beetles (Carabidae, excl. cicindelinae) of Canada and Alaska* (in 6 parts), by Carl H. Lindroth,[18] and *The Carabid Beetles of Newfoundland*, also by Lindroth.[19] Each geographical region will require a different set of reference tools. The fossil beetle expert will also consult handbooks to help with preliminary identification of other fossil insects, seeds, nuts, snails, and so on that are found with the fossil beetles, although specialists in those areas will also be consulted especially for important or controversial findings.

Examples of handbooks used by Quaternary researchers interested in soils include *Methods of Soil Analysis*, 3rd ed.,[20] and *Minerals in Soil Environments*, 2nd ed.[21] Examples of encyclopedias that might be consulted by Quaternary researchers include *The Encyclopedia of Sedimentology*[22] and *Encyclopedia of Geomorphology.*[23]

Textbooks

One excellent textbook for QR is *Reconstructing Quaternary Environments*, 2nd ed.[24] This resource contains a lengthy bibliography that is a good resource in itself. There are many textbooks specific to the various subdisciplines related to QR.

Field Trip Guidebooks

Field trip guidebooks are rich information resources. Field trips are often held in conjunction with society meetings, and leaders generally provide guides for the participants. These guides can be anything from illustrations copied from other publications (sometimes without permission) and stapled together, handouts at each stop, or more formal, bound publications. Most contain a road log so that the trip can be replicated. Field trip guidebooks are important for several reasons. They often contain excellent background information for the trip area. When putting together a field trip, consulting guidebooks from previous trips can reduce the amount of work for the trip leader. In addition, over time many of the features have been, or will be mined out of existence, covered with concrete, asphalt, or buildings, or made inaccessible by owners. Field guides are valuable as records of ephemeral features such as moraines, dunes, beaches, and channel fill.

Indexes

The various online and print indexes are essential for efficient identification of literature. Since QR is strongly interdisciplinary, it may be necessary to use a number of indexes to find the majority of needed information and to determine the types of information covered by the various databases. For example, several may be necessary to search for information related to geoarchaeology, or for biological information, or for geochemistry.

Data Sets

Subdisciplines within QR accumulate data during the course of research. Increasingly, data sets are being made available via the Internet, or at least their existence and availability are more apparent due to the use of meta-data and the Internet.

Laboratories

Laboratories are important for several reasons. Laboratories often have collections that are used for comparative study. For example, an entomology laboratory will have a large collection of identified insects, and other labs may have core collections. Quaternary researchers may visit labs to compare their samples, or they may send their samples to a lab for identification or analysis. Other laboratories specialize in dating of samples by dendrochronology (tree ring analysis), isotope analysis, luminescence analysis, or other methods.

Experts in the Field

People are significant information resources. It is important to be able to identify and find other specialists in an area and specialists in related areas. Many societies maintain directories either in print or online; however, some restrict access to members only.

Electronic Discussion Lists

Electronic discussion lists are great information resources. By subscribing to various lists related to QR, a researcher or scholar can monitor discussions of ongoing research and learn about conferences, publications, and job opportunities. They are generally good places to post questions, although it is wise to exhaust other resources rather than cluttering up researchers' electronic mailboxes with easily answered questions.

SEARCHING FOR INFORMATION
RELATED TO QUATERNARY RESEARCH

The need for information can fall into two different categories. In some cases, the need involves discovering what information exists on a particular topic. In other cases, a particular article or document is sought with only a partial or inaccurate citation. The two different types of information needs require different search strategies, and for both there are usually multiple starting points and processes. In all cases, one starts with the known. The more that is known about the particular subject area and how information is found for that discipline, the general structure of literature in that area, and the research and publication process for scholarly information, the easier the task and the greater the likelihood of success. Literature searching involves skills that are honed through practice, and these skills are transferable from one discipline to another.

Strategies for Finding and Obtaining Journal Articles

Using Indexes to Find Articles

With the advent of online indexes, searching for journal articles has become much more efficient. As with all interdisciplinary subjects, no one index contains all the information related to QR. Whether attempting to determine what information exists for a topic within QR or trying to find a specific article, it may be necessary to consult a number of relevant online indexes.

A research project comparing eleven online indexes for QR has recently been completed (see Note 1). The eleven databases (*AGRICOLA, AGRIS, Aquatic Science and Fisheries Abstracts, Biological and Agricultural Index, Biological Abstracts, CAB Abstracts, Current Contents, GEOBASE, GeoRef, Water Resources Abstracts,* and *Zoological Record*) were searched for the publication year 2000 using the terms "Quaternary or Pleistocene or Holocene." A combined total of 12,896 records from all eleven databases were recovered. The top three databases for total relevant records were *GeoRef, GEOBASE,* and *Current Contents.* Most significantly, every index contained unique records—information not included in any of the other databases that would have been missed had the index not been searched.

It is important to remember that indexes vary by the time period covered, the journal titles included, and the types of information included. For example, *GeoRef* indexes North American information back to 1785 and worldwide information back to 1933. Even so, not every piece of geological information for those time periods will be included. Some indexes such as *GeoRef* index government documents, book chapters, abstracts, conference papers, and maps, in addition to journal articles. Other indexes may only include article information. The speed at which materials are added also varies from index to index. All of these factors should be considered when using indexes to find information.

The enhanced search capabilities are even more useful for finding an elusive article from a bad reference. The first step is to determine which indexes would most likely help to identify the citation by considering the probable date of the article versus the date range covered by the index and the subject areas and journals covered by the index. After selecting the most promising index, use an advanced search mode and use the known information to search by fields. Common errors in references often include an incorrect publication date, errors in the spelling of the author's name, incorrect volume or page numbers, and incorrect journal name. The correct article can often be found by varying the information searched. For example, an incorrect publication date can be countered by leaving out that information or by entering a date range rather than a single year. An incorrect author or misspelled name can be worked around by leaving out the author name in the search. Variations in spelling can be countered by using truncation symbols (e.g., "pal*eontology" to search for both the American and British forms of the word), and truncation symbols can be used if one is uncertain whether a word is plural or singular or takes some other form after the root. In some cases, albeit rare, articles are cited (usually designated "in press") but are never actually published.

Using Other Sources to Find and Obtain Articles

Sometimes the best resources for finding information are people. See the discussion below for strategies that can be used to find individuals. Experts in a subdiscipline of QR can be consulted to determine the most relevant information. Individuals may also be the best resource for finding and obtaining copies of known but elusive articles. The authors may be able to confirm whether an article was actually published and may be able to provide a copy of the article. Also, do not hesitate to consult a subject librarian for help identifying and obtaining information. Electronic discussion lists are another resource for finding and obtaining elusive information.

Articles in journals not held by your institution's library are often available via interlibrary borrowing or document delivery (i.e., the article is purchased from specialized vendors). Costs for these services may or may not be absorbed by the library, depending on your institution's policies. Alternatively, you may want to visit another library to access the literature. The worldwide catalog *WorldCat* can be used to find the libraries that own particular journals.

With the advent of electronic journals, whole collections of journals can be searched for information via publishers' or aggregators' Internet pages. Several geological organizations are in the process of introducing *Geo-ScienceWorld*, an aggregation of online geological journals (www.geosociety.org/news/pr/04-03.htm).

Strategies for Finding Older Journal Literature

Finding older information, especially in non-English languages, can be particularly difficult. Although *GeoRef* indexes information published in North America back to 1785, coverage is not exhaustive. *GeoRef* only indexes worldwide information back to 1933. The lack of abstracts in older *GeoRef* records further limits the ability to recover older information. Most other on-line indexes related to QR do not go back as far as *GeoRef*.

As the full texts of journals are retrospectively scanned and made available on the Internet, additional, older information will come to light. Examples include the ability to search older journals such as *Philosophical Transactions of the Royal Society of London, Proceedings of the National Academy of Sciences of the United States of America 1915–2001, Science,* and *American Journal of Science*. The Royal Society's *Catalogue of Scientific Papers 1800–1900* is being added to the *19th Century Masterfile* database. Again, consult subject librarians at various institutions for help with older and non-English literature.

Several reference books that may help you find appropriate print indexes are *Geology Emerging*[25] and *Geologic Reference Sources*, 2nd ed.[26] Mary W. Scott has identified a number of print indexes that cover pre-1900 geologic literature.[27] Much of this literature is not included in *GeoRef* or any other online index. In addition, according to Scott, "The Geological Society's library in 1895 lists 299 serial titles that they received that year." Any or all of these journals could contain information relevant for QR, and much of the material is probably not contained in any online index. Unless or until the older literature is indexed in online databases and/or made available in full-text online, most of the information will remain hidden and will only be "unearthed" with time-consuming, diligent effort.

Strategies for Finding Other Research Material

Diane K. Baclawski has demonstrated the problems inherent in older, dispersed collections of research materials left by scientists by considering the glacial studies materials left by Frank Leverett and Frank Taylor.[28] These materials include U.S. Geological Survey Monograph 53, *The Pleistocene of Indiana and Michigan and the History of the Great Lakes,* published in 1915, and currently only available in the original. In addition, they left behind field notebooks, letters, maps, and other materials that are available for inspection only in diverse places. This case study illustrates the difficulty of identifying, finding, and gaining access to important older information and also the necessity of preserving and providing access to it. Perhaps in trying to find these types of materials, it is best to start by contacting librarians at the government agencies and at university libraries within the geographic area of the original research.

People

Individuals are great resources for finding general information, obtaining articles, finding data sets and laboratories, and for finding other individuals.

Use online indexes such as *GeoRef* and *Current Contents* to find authors. Some indexes include author addresses and other contact information. Ask on an electronic discussion list. Use online society directories.[29] Find names using *Dissertation Abstracts* and pursue the authors using Internet search engines, such as Google, to find current contact information.

Handbooks and Other Monographs

Identifying relevant handbooks can be difficult. Often, the term "handbook" is not a part of the title. The following are similar terms to use: manual, methods, taxonomy, classification, analysis, testing, or field description. Do not forget to use synonyms and related terms, (e.g., "soil* or pedology or paleosoil* or paleopedology"). *WorldCat* is an excellent online index to search for handbooks, encyclopedias, and other monographs. This resource not only provides the ability to search libraries worldwide, but also lists the libraries that hold the resource. Other databases to search include commercial Internet websites, such as amazon.com and barnesandnoble.com, or the publications pages of various organizations. Links to many publishers and dealers can be found at www.library.uiuc.edu/gex/bookpubs.html. A searchable index of earth science-related book reviews can be found at g118.grainger.uiuc.edu/gexbookreviews/reviews. Finally, the best resources for finding the exact needed reference may still be individual experts, electronic discussion lists, or subject librarians.

Field Trip Guidebooks

As previously mentioned, field trip guidebooks are difficult to identify and obtain. Previously, coverage of field trip guidebooks in the *GeoRef* database was rather incomplete. Through the combined efforts of the GeoRef staff and members of Geoscience Information Society, more of these titles are being included in *GeoRef*. Another resource is the *Union List of Geologic Field Trip Guidebooks of North America*, 6th ed.[30] The free, online version of this resource is continually updated (www.agiweb.org/georef/onlinedb/gnaintro.html). Other resources for identifying and locating field trip guidebooks are the Online Computer Library Center's *WorldCat* database (www.oclc.org/worldcat), a worldwide library union catalog, and the web pages of the various associations, societies, and agencies. Some guidebooks are now being posted on the Internet, at least temporarily. Attending the field trip may be the best way to obtain a copy of a specific guide. For example, it is very difficult to obtain a guide book from most Friends of the Pleistocene field trips without participating in the trip.

When searching *GeoRef* or *WorldCat* for field trip guidebooks, be aware that the words sometimes appear separately in the guidebook title (i.e., "field trip guide book"), and sometimes they are combined ("fieldtrip guidebook"), so multiple searches or the use of truncation symbols may be necessary in order find the appropriate resource. Other terms to search in combination with the previous terms include the geographic location (e.g., Death Valley), county, state, and/or region. An example of a search is (field*trip or guide*book) and (Death Valley) and (Pleistocene or Quaternary).

Indexes

The top three indexes for QR in general are *GeoRef, GEOBASE,* and *Current Contents.*[31] Others can be found by consulting the Internet websites of libraries at major universities. Another resource is the *Worldwide Database Catalogue* of The DIALOG Corporation, which is available in print or on DIALOG's website (www.dialog.com). Brief information and coverage is given for the majority of the commercial online indexes in existence. Nearly all of the online indexes are by subscription only. Many are available at university libraries.

Data Sets

Quaternary researchers may need to know which data sets are available for use or comparison. Often the best resources are individual contacts found by attending conferences, reading the literature, inquiring on electronic discussion lists, or searching the Internet websites of institutions, associations, agencies, and individuals. For some Internet resources for finding data sets, see Lura E. Joseph.[32] One resource is NASA's *Global Change Master Directory* (ds.datastarweb.com/ds/products/datastar/ds.htm), a directory of earth science data and services.

Images

Quaternary researchers may need images to illustrate publications and presentations at conferences. They often produce their own images, but if that is not practical, other sources are available. In nearly all cases, it is necessary to gain permission to use images produced by others. Sources of images include illustrations in journals and monographs and documents on the Internet. The Internet search engines Google and AltaVista offer the ability to search for images only.[33]

Dissertations

Several ways to search for dissertations include *GeoRef,* UMI/Proquest's *Digital Dissertations* (www.umi.com/umi/dissertations/), and *WorldCat.*

Many dissertations can be purchased from Proquest. It is possible to download the full text of dissertations and theses published after 1996, and for authorized users from participating institutions, the downloaded copies are free. Information about Canadian theses and dissertations can be found at www.collectionscanada.ca/6/4/index-e.html.

Conference Proceedings

Conference proceedings and transactions are important sources of current information. Research may be presented at conferences well in advance of publication in journals. Indeed, some information found in proceedings may never be published in journals. Many libraries purchase conference proceedings. These can be found by searching university online catalogs and *WorldCat*.

Meetings

The best places to find out about upcoming meetings and conferences are at the Internet websites of associations, in newsletters, on electronic discussion lists, and in current journals. Calls for papers can be found in the same sources as for meetings notifications. In addition, the database *Call for Papers* (www.papersinvited.com) can be searched.

Biographical Information

Some of the society publications contain biographical information, especially in relation to awards and obituaries. Check the appropriate newsletters and society Internet websites. Biographical information about Quaternary researchers may also be found in publications such as *Geoscientist, Geotimes, Geology Today, Geoscience Canada*, and *EOS*. It is worth checking the various online and print biographical indexes such as *Biography and Genealogy Master Index* and *American National Biography*.

Current Awareness

Maintaining current awareness of the literature and research in an extremely interdisciplinary subject such as QR is a formidable task. Tools such as *Current Contents* can help. The *Current Contents* interface provides the ability to save searches and repeat them periodically. The database is interdisciplinary, which is very helpful for QR searches. Some publishers are now offering tables-of-contents services and will periodically send e-mail information based on a list of journals or a list of topics or keywords. Another option is to periodically search selected electronic journals or other indexes. Other ways to stay current with information include attending conferences, looking through conference proceedings, and networking with other researchers.

Organizing Information

Re-finding information can sometimes be even more difficult than finding it in the first place. With the increasing amount of information, and the variety of formats, managing information is increasingly difficult. With the increase in electronic journals, tables-of-contents services, and citation software, new solutions for information management are possible; however, most are still time consuming.

CONCLUSION

QR is an extremely interdisciplinary area with information "tentacles" reaching back to the beginnings of geology and into a wide variety of other sciences. The field is of particular current importance to society due to an emphasis on climate and environmental change research. QR is preserved and fostered as an integrated discipline by a strong international organization; many related national, regional, and local organizations; and journals and other serials devoted to QR. Search strategies for QR information are similar to those for other interdisciplinary sciences. Knowledge of basic search strategies is necessary, but it is also necessary to be cognizant of the structure of the QR literature, the related sciences that make up QR, and the relevant online and print indexes. Finally, some sort of personal method of information management is necessary for efficient research.

NOTES

1. The information in this introductory section closely follows the introductory section in a journal article by the same author with the working title, "Comparison of Retrieval Performance of Eleven Online Indexes Used for Quaternary Research, an Interdisciplinary Study Area," conditionally accepted for publication.

2. S. C. Porter, "Quaternary Science," *INQUA Brochure*, www.inqua.tcd.ie/brochure/brochure.htm (accessed April 21, 2004); D. Dryer, "The American Quaternary Association," www4.nau.edu/amqua/default.asp (accessed April 21, 2004).

3. J. J. Clague, "Revision of the Geological Time Scale: Implications for the Quaternary," e-mail communication, June 16, 2004).

4. J. G. Ogg, "Status of Divisions of the International Geologic Time Scale," *Letha* 37, no. 1 (2004): 184–99; F. M. Gradstein and J. G. Ogg, "Geologic Time Scale 2004: Why, How, and Where Next!" *Lethaia* 37, no. 2 (2004): 176–81.

5. S. C. Porter, "Quaternary Science."

6. S. C. Porter, "Quaternary Science."

7. N. I. Nikolaev, "Current State and Prospects of Quaternary Research," *Moscow University Geology Bulletin* 54, no. 1 (1999): 1–10.

8. H. L. Levin, *The Earth Through Time*, 5th ed. (New York: Saunders College Publishing, 1996), 23, 498–99. For a more extensive discussion of the history of the use of the term "Quaternary," see R. F. Flint, "Introduction" in Kalervo Rankama, ed., *The Quaternary*, vol. 1 (New York: Interscience Publishers, 1965), xi–xxii.

9. Quaternary Research Association, "What is the Quaternary?" September 13, 2000, at gra.org.uk/what.html (accessed July 18, 2004).

10. Nikolaev, "Current State and Prospects of Quaternary Research."

11. S. C. Porter, "Quaternary Science."

12. Scripps Institution of Oceanography, *Initial Reports of the Deep Sea Drilling Project* 1 (Washington, DC: Scripps Institution of Oceanography, 1968), vii.

13. C. Hammer and others, "Preface," *Journal of Geophysical Research* 102, no. C12 (1997): 26, 315–16.

14. Laurent Augustin and others, "Eight glacial cycles from an Antarctic ice core," *Nature* 429 (Jun 10, 2004): 623–28.

15. Leon Follmer, Illinois State Geological Survey, personal communication.

16. Lura E. Joseph, "Associations & Information Resources for Quaternary Research," July 3, 2006, at www.library.uiuc.edu/gex/bibs/QuaternaryInformation Resources.html (accessed September 26, 2004).

17. Joseph, "Associations & Information Resources for Quaternary Research."

18. Carl H. Lindroth, *The Ground-Beetles (Carabidae, excl. Cicindelinae) of Canada and Alaska*, 6 vols., *Opuscula Entomologica* suppl. 35, 20, 24, 29, 33, 34 (Entomologiska Sallskapet, 1969, 1963, 1966 1968, 1969).

19. Carl H. Lindroth, *The Carabid Beetles of Newfoundland; Including the French Islands St. Pierre and Miquelon, Opuscula Entomologica* Suppl. 12 (Entomologiska Sallskapet, 1955).

20. Arnold Klute and others, *Methods of Soil Analysis*, 3rd ed., 3 vols. (Madison, WI: Soil Science Society of America, 1994–1996).

21. J. B. Dixon, S. B. Weed, and R. C. Dinauer, *Minerals in Soil Environments*, 2nd ed. (Madison, WI: Soil Science Society of America, 1989).

22. R. W. Fairbridge and J. Bourgeois, eds., *The Encyclopedia of Sedimentology* (New York: Academic Press, 1978).

23. A. Goudie, *Encyclopedia of Geomorphology*, 2 vols. (New York: Routledge/ International Association of Geomorphologists, 2004).

24. J. J. Lowe and M. J. C. Walker, *Reconstructing Quaternary Environments*, 2nd ed. (Essex, GB: Addison Wesley Longman Limited, 1997).

25. D. C. Ward, and A. V. Carozzi, *Geology Emerging: A Catalog Illustrating the History of Geology (1500–1850) from a Collection in the Library of the University of Illinois at Urbana-Champaign* (Urbana, IL: University of Illinois Library, 1984).

26. D. W. Ward, M. W. Wheeler, and R. A. Bier Jr., 1981, *Geological Reference Sources*, 2nd ed. (Metuchen, NJ: Scarecrow Press, Inc., 1981).

27. Mary W. Scott, "Status of Bibliographic Control of Pre-1900 Geoscience Literature," in *Geoscience Information Society Proceedings* (Alexandria, VA: Geoscience Information Society, 2004), 105–8.

28. Diane K. Baclawski, "Making the Past Come Alive: Bringing Leverett & Taylor & USGS Monograph 53 to the 21st Century," in *Geoscience Information Society Proceedings* (Alexandria, VA: Geoscience Information Society, 2004), 109–14.

29. See Lura E. Joseph, "Associations & Information Resources for Quaternary Research" for sources of online society directories.

30. Geoscience Information Society Guidebooks Committee, *Union List of Geologic Field Trip Guidebooks of North America*, 6th ed. (Alexandria, VA: American Geological Institute, 1996).

31. For most of the online indexes relevant for Quaternary Research, see Lura E. Joseph, "Associations & Information Resources for Quaternary Research."

32. See Lura E. Joseph, "Associations & Information Resources for Quaternary Research" for other sources of data sets.

33. See Lura E. Joseph, "Associations & Information Resources for Quaternary Research" for other sources of image collections.

4

Human Factors Engineering

Linda G. Ackerson and Anna Berkes

Human factors engineering pairs measurement and function to design systems in which humans interact with machines or equipment, physical environments, and the tasks that compose the system. It is a design methodology to ensure safety, worker satisfaction, and productivity.[1] The design of systems involves two components. The first is the environment, which could be an enclosed space, such as a school, hospital, or airplane cockpit. An environment could also be an open system such as transportation routes in an urban neighborhood. The second component of systems design is human characteristics, including anatomical and biomechanical data.

HISTORY AND DEVELOPMENT

Beginning in the 1940s during World War II and continuing into the 1950s, human factors engineering was primarily applied in the United States to solve military problems. Military personnel concluded that many weapon systems failed because of human error. Upon further inspection, it became apparent that the design of the weapon itself greatly contributed to operator inefficiency, because the weapon system was not designed to include humans as part of the system.[2] This observation proved to be the precipitating event that caused the disciplines of engineering and psychology to combine and form the interdisciplinary field of human factors.

This time period is widely known as the "period of knobs and dials," in which emphasis was placed on the design of instrument panels and control knobs to maximize efficiency between human-machine interaction.[3] Tests

of air combat situations demonstrated that the specific design and place-
ment of sensors and controls were not as important as the total environment in which the air crew resided.

The subject terms "human factors" and "ergonomics" are often used interchangeably, but they differ in the focus of research.[4] During the 1950s,
increased automation led to growth in manufacturing. Great Britain used
physiological factors, such as biomechanics, to develop an effective work
flow system. The European model, which uses the term ergonomics, stresses
the concept of human energy and performance. In contrast, the American
model, which uses the term human factors, favors a psychological approach
that stresses information processing.

Several support systems sustain research and project development involving human factors engineering. Federal funding provided the most significant level of support. Wartime research that began in the United States
during the mid-1940s resulted in the establishment and continued funding
of military laboratories. In the 1960s, federal agencies began to sponsor
projects involving civilian activities, such as the design of roadways and air
traffic control.[5] The Navy and Air Force contracted for engineering psychology research at major universities, notably Johns Hopkins University, Harvard University, Tufts University, Rochester Institute of Technology, University of Maryland, University of Washington, Mount Holyoke, and University
of California, Berkeley.[6]

Professional societies also sustain research on human factors engineering. In 1949, the Ergonomics Research Society formed in Great Britain. It
provided a forum for the development and discussion of common interests
among psychologists, physiologists, physicists, engineers, and physicians. In
1954, the Human Factors Society formed in the United States, followed by
the Human Factors and Ergonomics Society in 1957. The International Ergonomics Association became a formal organization in 1958. All three associations distribute journals and newsletters to keep their members informed of each others' activities and encourage collaboration.[7]

STRUCTURE OF HUMAN FACTORS LITERATURE

Journal Articles and Conference Proceedings

The most effective method of searching for articles and conference papers
published in the engineering literature is to use *Engineering Index*. The
equivalent database is *Compendex*. Many of the earliest studies on human
factors originated in industrial engineering and were concerned with the
production and distribution of goods.[8] To locate literature published from
1918 through 1939, researchers should search for the following subject

terms: industrial management, industrial psychology, industrial welfare, and human engineering. However, subject terms change over time as the field matures, and a current authority guide to terminology is helpful for locating articles that would have been missed by limiting the search to the older terms specified here. The most current subject guide for *Compendex* is *Ei Thesaurus*.[9]

Psychological Abstracts is the best source for finding articles and conference papers in the psychology literature. The equivalent database is *PsycINFO*. From 1967 to 2005, search for the following subject terms: applied psychology, engineering psychology, human factors, and human engineering. The authority guide for *PsycINFO* is the *Thesaurus of Psychological Index Terms*.[10] Most of the earlier literature on human factors was written in English, and it is difficult to find articles published in other languages. Significant research on human factors engineering was conducted in Europe during the early 1900s and in Asia in the 1970s. In 1975, the Korean Research Standards Institute was established to improve technology for precise anthropometric measurement.[11] Both *Engineering Index* and *Psychological Abstracts* are international in scope, so they include citations to articles published in other languages.

Government and Laboratory Reports

A great deal of human factors literature is published in the form of government and laboratory reports. Reports are marginally covered in the article indexes, but bibliographies are more effective in finding them. Bibliographies help to gather unnumbered report series that would otherwise be separated in the literature.

Some reports from World War II were classified because they contain sensitive or secret data. These reports include, but are not limited to, information on the development and testing of military weapon systems and those concerning psychological activities. They were often labeled "restricted" because they discussed military equipment, but were later declassified. The U.S. Department of Defense has developed guidelines about when and what type of materials will be declassified.[12] Department of Defense information that is believed to be of permanent value is deposited in the U.S. National Archives. The archivist and Department of Defense representatives review classified reports after they are thirty years old to assess their potential for national security risks. Series containing intelligence activities, sources, and methods that were created after 1945 are reviewed after fifty years. After thirty to fifty years, almost all of these reports are declassified. The National Technical Information Service, a documents repository for government-sponsored research that is maintained by the Department of Commerce, can verify whether a classified document has been declassified.

A major source for locating older journal and report literature on human factors engineering is the Human Engineering Bibliography series compiled by Tufts University.[13] This series of bibliographies is the result of a contract with the Office of Naval Research to gather information that could be used for the development of military equipment. The first in the series collected the citations to information published in journals, symposia proceedings, and reports from government, industrial, and university laboratories that had been published from 1950 to 1955. Researchers should consult the index that accompanies the bibliography to obtain its maximum value.[14] The last of four additional bibliographies in this series was published in 1962, covering additions to the literature from 1959 to 1961.[15]

Statistical Data

Three types of data on human characteristics are used in design. The first is anthropometric measurements of human anatomy and body dimensions. Traditional static measurements include height, breadth, depth, distance, curvature, circumference, and reach.[16] The second type is dynamic biomechanical data, such as strength-endurance relationship, lift and grip capacity, and fatigue-recovery rates.[17] The third type is psychological data. The *Engineering Data Compendium*, a massive three-volume set, is the most complete collection of statistics on human perception and performance.[18] Visual, auditory, and tactile data in this source were gathered during the 1960s to the 1980s.

The earliest measurements of body dimensions are of military populations, because of the focus on military equipment. However, the body dimensions of military personnel will be more restrictive, whereas individuals in industrial settings will be more representative of the general population. Over time, the general population becomes more diverse, because characteristics of population groups, such as age, gender, and ethnicity, change. It is crucial to use the most current data that reflect a larger segment of the population.

Baseline data are abundant. The National Aeronautics and Space Administration Reference Publication 1024 provides the most comprehensive source of anthropometric data up through 1978, representing measurements taken during the 1950s to the 1970s.[19] The most readily available source of updated data on the American population is from U.S. government agencies and laboratories. For example, the U.S. Department of Health, Education, and Welfare publishes the Vital and Health Statistics series. The best strategy for locating current information gathered by government agencies is to search the *Catalog of United States Government Publications*, which is available on the Internet at www.gpoaccess.gov.

Data in the *Statistical Abstract of the United States* are derived primarily from information compiled by the U.S. Census Bureau.[20] This source provides detailed data tables on the American population in terms of growth, distribution, and characteristics, such as the size of the Hispanic population in the United States, geographic mobility, and average household income. Changes in population characteristics, such as age, gender, and ethnicity, over the next twenty to fifty years are projected.

Standards, Guidelines, and Regulations

Human factors engineers are legally obligated to follow government standards specified in the U.S. Code of Federal Regulations (CFR). The CFR are rules issued by the Executive departments and agencies of the federal government. Regulations are evaluated and revisions are made annually as needed. Engineers should look for changes before they begin the design project. For example, the Occupational Safety and Health Administration (OSHA) is responsible for the oversight of regulations regarding health and safety in the workplace. The rules for this regulation can be found in 29 CFR Part 1910. OSHA standards are occasionally revised, and the most recent updates are available at www.osha.gov.

The *Human Engineering Guide to Equipment Design* was a major source of information for the design of physical environments when it was first published in 1963.[21] Although the original purpose of the guide was to specify design principles for military applications, it was later adopted for industrial settings, because it illustrated the basic principles of workplace dimensions and layout. The guide was revised in 1972, but much of the data were taken during the 1960s. Passage of the Americans with Disabilities Act (ADA) in 1990 created the ADA Standards for Accessible Design to regulate the design and construction of public buildings. These standards are coded in 28 CFR Part 36, and first notice of revisions is posted at the ADA website at www.ada.gov.

FUTURE DIRECTIONS IN HUMAN FACTORS ENGINEERING

The concept of macroergonomics will be a significant trend in the next decade.[22] Traditional human factors design is based on human-computer interaction, which involves people and technology. Macroergonomics is the design of systems that feature organization and management. These systems are composed of tasks, human interaction with software and hardware, and the factors that affect the larger environment, such as temperature, illumination, and noise. Macroergonomics is particularly applicable to industrial settings.

Community ergonomics uses human factors principles and human behavioral characteristics for assessment at the societal level.[23] Community ergonomics has been successfully applied to inner cities that suffer from social isolation. In inner cities, people are often separated from health care facilities, schools, fire departments, and businesses because of location. Community ergonomics designers assess the needs of the community and identify support services required, such as public transportation systems.

Neuroergonomics is a relatively new concept, with most of the research in this area ranging from 1997 to 2003.[24] Neuroergonomics can be applied to the design of systems that have a strong human-machine interface and build on neuroscience. The challenge for engineers in this area is to develop sophisticated ways of measuring human information processing and to use the continuous flow of information to link to machines that adapt to the operator's thought processes or actions. Individuals with physical disabilities would be able to use this computer-based system to perform activities they would otherwise be unable to do.

Human factors principles will play a significant role in the improvement of health care facilities over the next decade.[25] Patient safety will be a primary concern. In addition, human factors engineering will aid in the design of prosthetics and other medical devices and instruments.

NOTES

1. Martin G. Helander, "Forty Years of IEA: Some Reflections on the Evolution of Ergonomics," *Ergonomics* 40, no. 10 (October 1997): 958.

2. Walter F. Grether, "Engineering Psychology in the United States," *American Psychologist* 23, no. 10 (October 1968): 743–44.

3. K. H. E. Kroemer, "Arbeitswissenschaft," *Werkstattstechnik* 60, no. 8 (August 1956): 472. This article was translated from German to English by Anna Berkes, May 2005.

4. Alphonse Chapanis, "Engineering Psychology," in *Annual Review of Psychology* (Palo Alto, CA: Annual Reviews, Inc., 1963), 287.

5. Martin G. Helander, " The Human Factors Profession," in *Handbook of Human Factors and Ergonomics*, ed. Gavriel Salvendy, 2nd. ed. (New York: Wiley, 1997), 5.

6. Grether, "Engineering Psychology in the United States," 744.

7. Frederic Bartlett, "Bearing of Medicine and Psychology on Engineering," *Chartered Mechanical Engineer* 8, no. 5 (May 1961): 297–99.

8. Kroemer, "Arbeitswissenschaft," 473.

9. Jessica L. Milstead, ed., *Ei Thesaurus*, rev. 4th ed. (Hoboken, NJ: Engineering Information, Inc., 2001.) *Ei Thesaurus* has been the official thesaurus since 1993. Prior to 1993, the thesaurus was titled *SHE, Subject Headings in Engineering*.

10. Lisa A. Gallagher, ed., *Thesaurus of Psychological Index Terms*, 10th ed. (Washington, DC: American Psychological Association, 2005).

11. M. Kumashiro and E. D. Megaw, eds., *Towards Human Work: Solutions to Problems in Occupational Health and Safety* (Bristol, PA: Taylor & Francis, 1991), 35–41.

12. D. Whitman, *"Guidelines for Systematic Declassification Review of Classified Information in Permanently Valuable DoD Records* (Washington, DC: Government Printing Office, 1983) NTIS, AD-A272 463. Microfiche.

13. Chapanis, "Engineering Psychology," 288.

14. Donald B. Devoe and Ezra V. Saul, "The Tufts Index to Human Engineering Literature," *Human Factors* 1, no. 4 (November 1959): 47–54.

15. Margaret Gooch, Librarian, Tisch Library, Tufts University, e-mail conversation with author, August 4, 2004.

16. K. H. E. Kroemer, "Engineering Anthropometry," *Ergonomics* 32, no. 7 (July 1989): 768.

17. William S. Marras, "Biomechanics of the Human Body," in *Handbook of Human Factors and Ergonomics*, ed. Gavriel Salvendy, 2nd ed. (New York: Wiley, 1997), 233–67.

18. Kenneth R. Boff and Janet E. Lincoln, *Engineering Data Compendium: Human Perception and Performance*, 3 vols. (Wright-Patterson Air Force Base: Harry G. Armstrong Aerospace Medical Research Laboratory, 1988).

19. Webb Associates, *Anthropometric Source Book, NASA Reference Publication 1024*, 3 vols. (Washington, DC: National Aeronautics and Space Administration, 1978).

20. U.S. Bureau of the Census. *Statistical Abstract of the United States*, 124th ed. (Washington, DC: Government Printing Office, 2004–2005).

21. Clifford T. Morgan and others, eds., *Human Engineering Guide to Equipment Design* (New York: McGraw-Hill, 1963).

22. Hal W. Hendrick, "An Overview of Macroergonomics," in *Macroergonomics: Theory, Methods, and Applications*, ed. Hal W. Hendrick and Brian M. Kleiner (Mahwah, NJ: Lawrence Earlbaum Associates, 2002), 1–23.

23. John Henry Smith and others, "Community Ergonomics," in *Macroergonomics: Theory, Methods, and Applications*, ed. Hal W. Hendrick and Brian M. Kleiner (Mahwah, NJ: Lawrence Earlbaum Associates, 2002), 289–309.

24. P. A. Hancock and J. L. Szalma, "The Future of Neuroergonomics," *Theoretical Issues in Ergonomics Science* 44, no. 1/2 (January-June 2003): 238–49.

25. Lucian L. Leape, "Human Factors Meets Health Care: The Ultimate Challenge," *Ergonomics in Design* 12, no. 3 (Summer 2004): 6–12.

5

Nanotechnology

Teresa U. Berry and Jeanine Williamson

Although scientists have worked in the nanoscale world of atoms and molecules for over a century, nanotechnology is a relatively new field. The word "nano-technology" first appeared in 1974 when Norio Taniguchi, a researcher in ultra-fine machining at Tokyo Science University, described a "technology aimed to get the preciseness and fineness of 1 nm."[1] A nanometer is a billionth of a meter or about eighty thousand times smaller than the width of a human hair. However, nanotechnology has expanded to encompass more than the science of the very small and has come to mean different concepts to many people, thus making it difficult to define. Generally, it embodies research and development at the atomic or molecular level in the 1–100 nanometer range; the creation and use of structures, devices, and systems that exhibit novel properties and functions due to their nanoscale size; and the ability to control and manipulate at the atomic level.[2]

HISTORY AND DEVELOPMENT

The beginning of nanotechnology is often traced back to an after dinner speech given to the West Coast section of the American Physical Society in 1959. Renowned physicist Richard Feynman invited his listeners "to enter a new field of physics" exploring "the problem of manipulating and controlling things on a small scale." Calling miniaturization "the most primitive, halting step," Feynman believed a time would come when researchers would be able to manipulate individual atoms to synthesize a specific material or to build computers, motors, and other devices.[3]

In the 1970s, K. Eric Drexler, a student at the Massachusetts Institute of Technology, began to develop his own ideas of nanotechnology before he had heard of Feynman's speech. Whereas Feynman spoke of using progressively smaller machines to build molecular devices, Drexler proposed a "bottom-up" approach, in which molecular machines could be built atom-by-atom, much like the biochemical systems that synthesize proteins. In perhaps the first publication about nanotechnology, he outlined the general principles of molecular engineering technology in a 1981 article in the *Proceedings of the National Academy of Sciences.*[4] Five years later, he expanded his ideas in his book *Engines of Creation: The Coming Era in Nanotechnology,*[5] in which he describes a world with self-replicating nanomachines, cell repair devices that enter the bloodstream to combat disease and aging, and molecular assemblers that can build anything from rockets to food. That same year, Drexler and several of his colleagues founded the Foresight Institute, which provides information about the development of nanotechnology and its consequences. Although many viewed Drexler's ideas as science fiction, he is often credited with bringing nanotechnology to the forefront of public awareness.

Research in nanotechnology gained momentum after several key events occurred. The first important development was the invention of the scanning tunneling microscope in 1981 by Gerd Binnig and Heinrich Rohrer, physicists at IBM's Zurich Research Lab. The scanning tunneling microscope allowed scientists to observe structures at the nanometer scale and to see individual atoms of conductive materials. Five years later, Binnig, Calvin Quate, and Christoph Gerber invented the atomic force microscope, a modification of the scanning tunneling microscope that could be used with nonconductive materials. Although the scanning tunneling microscope and atomic force microscope were originally designed as imaging tools, a defining moment occurred in 1989 when IBM scientists used a scanning tunneling microscope to position individual xenon atoms in a pattern that spelled "IBM," thus opening the door to building structures from the "bottom-up" as Feynman and Drexler envisioned.

Another milestone in the history of nanotechnology occurred in 1985, when chemists Richard Smalley, Robert Curl, and Harold Kroto found evidence of a new form of carbon called fullerenes, which can occur as round balls or long tubes. Buckminsterfullerene, the first fullerene discovered, is a molecule consisting of sixty carbon atoms arranged in a spherical polyhedron structure and resembling the geodesic dome designed by the architect Buckminster Fuller. This discovery launched a new branch in chemistry, as scientists scrambled to understand the properties of these remarkable molecules and to find ways to synthesize and manipulate the structures. In 1991, Sumio Iijima discovered a simple and efficient method for creating nanotubes, which are essentially elongated fullerenes. Nanotubes proved to have incredible tensile strength and high superconductivity. Interest in nanotechnology escalated as researchers looked for applications for these novel structures.

Considered as the driving force for the next technological revolution, nanotechnology research and development exploded. In the late 1990s, several government studies surveyed the state of nanotechnology research in the world and concluded that the federal government needed to invest in nanoscale research in order for the United States to remain globally competitive. These reports also recognized the interdisciplinary nature of nanotechnology and emphasized the need to "create a new breed of researchers who can work across traditional boundaries."[6] In 2000, the National Nanotechnology Initiative was established to coordinate the efforts in nanoscale science, engineering, and technology among multiple federal agencies. Federal funding increased from $116 million in 1997 to $961 million in 2004.[7] This attitude towards nanoscale science is not restricted to the United States. Governments in several European and Asian countries also consider nanotechnology to be a national priority and started their own initiatives with similar funding increases.

Nanotechnology evolved from the parent disciplines of physics, chemistry, and engineering but uses the literature from many other disciplines as well. The influx of government funding created several nanoscale science and engineering research centers to foster interdisciplinary collaboration. However, in a bibliometric study of papers published in nanojournals, Joachim Schummer concluded that current nanoscale research is not particularly interdisciplinary. He viewed nanotechnology not as a single field, but as several different specialized subfields within the classical disciplines (i.e., nanotechnology is multidisciplinary rather than interdisciplinary).[8] The multidisciplinary aspect of nanotechnology is reflected by the fact that few nanotechnology societies exist independently. Instead, they tend to be divisions within established societies, such as the Nanometer-scale Science and Technology Division of the American Vacuum Society or the IEEE Nanotechnology Council of the Institute of Electrical and Electronics Engineers. This apparent lack of interdisciplinarity suggests that nanotechnology has not broken completely from its parent disciplines and is still emerging as a separate field.

STRUCTURE OF THE LITERATURE

The literature of nanotechnology is disseminated in five types of publications: journal articles, conference papers, books, government reports, and patents. The following is a discussion of effective search strategies for finding each type.

Journal Articles

Journal articles are the primary means of communicating research results and are often peer reviewed before publication. The first journal devoted to nanotechnology was published by the Institute of Physics. Launched in 1990, the original scope of *Nanotechnology* was principally atomic-level machining, metrology with nanosize dimensions, performance of micromechanisms in the design of instruments and machine tools, and applications of instruments such as scanning tunneling microscopes.[9] In 2002, *Nanotechnology* changed from a quarterly to a monthly publication and expanded its scope "to specifically cover research of an interdisciplinary nature."[10] Other societies began nanojournals, such as the American Chemical Society's *Nano Letters* in 2001 and *IEEE Transactions on Nanotechnology* in 2002. Some journals expanded their scope to include nanotechnology and changed their titles to reflect this trend, such as the *Journal of Vacuum Science & Technology B: Microelectronics and Nanometer Structures*. However, the majority of articles continue to be published in journals whose scopes are not restricted to nanoscale research. Although physics, chemistry, and engineering are the dominant disciplines in nanotechnology, there is a growing emphasis on life sciences, pharmacology, and medicine as reflected in the growth of nanoscience articles in journals in these fields and the appearance of new journals such as *IEEE Transactions on NanoBioscience* and *Nanomedicine: Nanotechnology, Biology and Medicine*.

With nanotechnology becoming an important research area in many disciplines, the number of publications has grown exponentially. Online bibliographic databases make literature searching easier, but sifting through a large number of citations can still be daunting. To give some idea of the volume, in 2003 *Science Citation Index* added over twenty thousand records containing a "nano" word.[11] This figure is a rough estimate since many nanotechnology papers do not have a "nano" term in the title or abstract, thus presenting a challenge to someone searching the literature. Another complicating factor is that database producers do not immediately incorporate new journals but wait to see if the impact of the new title warrants adding it to the database's coverage. For example, *Science Citation Index* does not include the first three years of the journal *Nanotechnology*.

When searching bibliographic databases, it is important for the user to understand the indexing policies of the database producer. Some databases use a standard list of vocabulary terms, or a thesaurus, to assign subject terms to each record, thus helping the searcher retrieve relevant citations without having to think of every possible synonym and spelling variation. The drawback to thesauri is the time lag between when a term appears in the literature and when the term is finally adopted in a thesaurus. *Inspec*, an important database for physics, electrical engineering, and computer science, began using the subject term "nanotechnology" in 1993, whereas the medical database *PubMed* did not adopt the term as a subject heading until 2002. Early developments in nanotechnology were often tied to microelectromechanical systems, so the searcher should not ignore "micro" subject terms, such as "micromechanical devices" or "microrobots," which predate "nano" terms.

For databases that do not use standardized vocabulary, retrieval is dependent on finding the words in the title and abstract of the database record. Searchers will need to compose a list of keywords taking into account the following:

1. synonyms (e.g., fullerene or buckminsterfullerene or C60)
2. acronyms (e.g., SWNTs or single-walled carbon nanotubes)
3. spelling variations such as plurals and British spelling (e.g., device or devices)
4. hyphenated/nonhyphenated words (e.g., C60 or C-60)

Truncation symbols will help retrieve word variants by allowing the searcher to enter a word stem, thus simplifying the search statement. However, a short word stem like "nano" will result in a number of irrelevant citations (e.g., the chemical formula $NaNO_3$).

Because nanotechnology research is interdisciplinary, this chapter discusses five scientific databases, including which Nanotechnology disciplines and topics are best covered by each one. It is often necessary to search multiple databases to ensure a comprehensive search. This chapter includes a few search tips for each database to aid researchers in performing an effective search. Databases vary in subject coverage, types of documents included (e.g., journal articles, technical reports, conference papers), and the range of publication years covered. These factors must be taken into account when choosing which databases to search.

Science Citation Index

Science Citation Index covers the articles and cited references of over 5,900 peer-reviewed journals published since 1945. *Science Citation Index* covers nanotechnology topics in a wide variety of disciplines including engineering, chemistry, and physics. Important subject terms associated with nanotechnology articles in the database include surfaces, films, nanoparticles, thin films, molecules, self-assembly, and fabrication. These subject terms show a breadth of nanotechnology research areas in this interdisciplinary database.

Search Tips

1. Make a list of possible keywords to use, including all possible synonyms, since *Science Citation Index* does not use a thesaurus to assign subject terms. Abstracts are not available prior to 1991, so retrieval of earlier citations is restricted to those with keywords appearing only in the article title. Search the other databases mentioned here to ensure a more comprehensive search of the earlier literature.
2. Take advantage of the "Cited Reference Search," where sources citing a relevant paper are obtained. This type of search makes it unnecessary to know terms that are used in an unfamiliar discipline, since the search methods include looking for specific authors or articles, as well as subjects.
3. Use the "Analyze" feature in the *Web of Science* interface to examine the characteristics of articles retrieved with nanotechnology searches. Articles may be ranked by author, document type, institution name, language, publication year, journal title, and subject. These rankings can give the searcher a good idea of the quality of his or her search as well as suggesting criteria to use in future searches.

Compendex

Compendex covers four hundred journals, key conference papers, and technical reports from all fields of engineering and applied science. Electronic coverage is available back to 1884. Topics in nanotechnology that are frequently found in *Compendex* are nanostructured materials, thin films, semiconducting silicon, microelectromechanical devices, electron beam lithography, masks, self-assembly, silicon, and semiconductor device manufacture.

Search Tips

1. Use the online thesaurus incorporated in the database to identify search terms within *Compendex*.
2. Supplement thesaurus searches with keyword searching in case thesaurus terms do not cover the time period or topic needed.

Inspec

Inspec covers over four thousand journals and two thousand published conference proceedings as well as books, reports, and dissertations from physics, computer science, electrical engineering, electronics and communications, and information technology. *Inspec* is more comprehensive in these areas than *Science Citation Index* and covers nanotechnology subjects primarily in electrical engineering and physics. Important subject descriptors in *Inspec* associated with nanotechnology records are nanostructured materials, silicon, atomic force microscopy, elemental semiconductors, transmission electron microscopy, scanning tunneling microscopy, self-assembly, scanning electron microscopy, and semiconductor growth. Although databases such as *Science Citation Index*, *Compendex*, and *Inspec* share coverage of some nanotechnology topics, it is worthwhile to search several databases, since they do not completely overlap.

Search Tips

1. Use the online thesaurus in *Inspec* as a source of search terminology.
2. Collect a list of keywords that may not have been incorporated in the thesaurus. Consider using "micro" and "molecular" terms (e.g., micromotors or molecular electronics) as well as related terms that imply nanosize, such as molecular wires or biolectronics, to improve retrieval of earlier literature.

SciFinder Scholar

SciFinder Scholar is the most comprehensive database for the chemical literature and covers over 8,000 journals dating back to 1907. It also includes patents, conference proceedings, books, dissertations, and more. A range of fields are associated with nanotechnology articles, from pharmaceutics to bioelectronics, biomaterials, biophysics, and electrical engineering. Important subject terms associated with nanotechnology articles are instrumentation, particle size, metabolism, crystallization, and chemical synthesis. Because *SciFinder Scholar* is such a large database, additional important subject terms are reported here: analysis, surface properties, DNA, polymers, materials testing, molecular conformation, microspheres, electrochemistry, and electron microscopy. Clearly, *SciFinder Scholar* covers many chemistry subjects relating to nanotechnology.

Search Tips

1. Enter any words in the "Research Topic" search. *SciFinder Scholar* accepts natural language queries and has an internal dictionary that will match synonyms and word variants automatically. Since the dictionary has limitations, enter alternative terms in parentheses (e.g., "growth (formation) of nanotubes").
2. Use the "Analyze/Refine" feature, multiple times if necessary, to narrow results further.

3. The earlier literature can be difficult to identify since chemists have always worked with nanosized materials. Relevant articles published before the 1980s use broad terms such as microspheres, particle size, carbon clusters, or aromatic hydrocarbons.

PubMed

PubMed is a free service offered by the National Library of Medicine at pubmed.gov. *PubMed* (MEDLINE) covers medical, nutrition, and clinical sciences and indexes more than 4,800 biomedical journals since 1951. Fields associated with nanotechnology articles are general science, chemistry, pharmaceutics, biomedical engineering, and biotechnology. Some of *PubMed*'s top subject headings from nanotechnology articles are particle size, molecular conformation, surface properties, crystallization methods, equipment design, macromolecular systems, and microspheres. Like *SciFinder Scholar*, *PubMed* covers several chemistry topics in nanotechnology articles. PubMed offers nanotechnology records likely to be useful to the pharmaceutical industry.

Search Tips

1. Browse the Medical Subject Headings (MeSH) to find appropriate terminology. The MeSH thesaurus is available at the website of the National Library of Medicine at www.nlm.nih.gov/mesh. Indexers assign the most specific headings to database records, but MeSH descriptors change over time as more specific terms are added. For example, the term "nanoparticles" was designated as a subject term for "nanostructures" in 2005, although the keyword began appearing in the database in 1978. Nanotechnology, a related term for "nanostructures," became an official MeSH descriptor in 2002. Before that, relevant articles can be found by searching for the MeSH heading "microchemistry" (1991–2001), "miniaturization" (1994–2001), and "electronics" (1966–1990). *PubMed* will automatically search for keywords in the current MeSH headings, but not to older or discontinued subject headings.
2. Limit the search to review articles to retrieve only overviews of your topic.
3. Search for related articles, which will lead to papers with similar subject headings and titles.

Conference Papers

Research results are often reported first in papers presented at scientific and engineering conferences; however, the proceedings can take up to two or more years to be published or may never be published at all. Nevertheless, conference proceedings are an important information resource. Conference papers on nanotechnology are listed in the bibliographic databases *Inspec*, *Compendex*, and *SciFinder Scholar*. To locate additional conference proceedings, search the database *WorldCat*, which aggregates library catalogs nationally and internationally. Nanotechnology conference papers are published by many engineering, physics, chemistry, and general scientific societies. To determine which societies issue nanotechnology conference proceedings, the user may search *WorldCat* and limit the document type to serial publications. Another approach is to search the subject term "congresses," a synonym for proceedings.

Books

Whereas journals and conferences are the primary sources of current information, books are excellent sources of information for those who need an overview of a topic or a state-of-the-art review. Nanotechnology topics are often covered in science and engineering encyclopedias and handbooks, but now "nano-titled" reference sources have also begun to appear. Your library's catalog will provide a list of books available in its collection, but you can also search other library collections through *WorldCat*. Some titles are available electronically for a fee, and it is sometimes possible to see excerpts through the publisher's website or the nascent Google Print (print.google.com).

Government Documents

Government documents report on the findings of nanotechnology research funded by Federal agencies. A good general search engine to use for locating nanotechnology websites is Google Government (www.google.com/unclesam), which reported more than 100,000 entries for nanotechnology research on July 12, 2005. Because this is such a large number of records to read, the user should combine search words with "AND," such as "Sandia AND Nanotechnology."

Another broad Internet website that links to government research on nanotechnology is the science.gov website (www.science.gov). The Internet websites located through this search were selected by twelve Federal agencies for inclusion in science.gov. The search default is to thirty resources, so the user may want to use the "Advanced Search," where he or she can retrieve more precise results by controlling the search parameters.

Two government agencies, the National Technical Information Service (NTIS) and the Office of Science and Technology Information (OSTI), are important sources of technical reports about nanotechnology. NTIS (www.ntis.gov) has a nanotechnology collection of more than 700 publications. The reports are not free but may be purchased online. OSTI's GrayLit Network (www.osti.gov/graylit) covers technical reports from the Department of Defense, Department of Energy, National Aeronautics and Space Administration, and the Environmental Protection Agency. Up to 250 records from each source may be retrieved. Some of the agencies incorporated in the GrayLit Network have full-text documents available. In addition to these sources, a searcher may want to visit a research library that serves as a federal depository library, since many technical reports may be included in the collection.

Patents

Patents serve as another important information resource of technological innovations in nanotechnology. Many nanotechnology patents are included at the U.S. Patent and Trademark Office website (www.uspto.gov). Nanotechnology patents are not grouped and can be found only through a keyword search. Users should search for their nanotechnology topics in the abstract, title, or description/specification, all of which will focus the search more than searching in all fields. After finding one relevant patent, the user should inspect the record for terms to use in a new search. In particular, the user should note the Current U.S. Classification numbers, so that he or she may expand the initial results by looking for patents classified the same way.

Worldwide patents may be found at the European Patent Office's Internet website (ep.espacenet.com). Select the "Worldwide" option to get the most comprehensive search. Note that there is an "Original Document" link that in some cases leads to full-text patents. Patents from more than seventy countries are included.

CONCLUSION

As nanotechnology continues to emerge within and across scientific disciplines, the researcher will need to be flexible and sensitive to new developments in other fields and aware of the subject terms that researchers are using to describe their nanotechnology inventions. Nanotechnology has a tradition of using whimsical names such as "buckyonions," "nanotube peapods," and "yolk shell nanostructures," but scientists are beginning to realize that a more methodical system is needed for naming new nanostructures.[12] In awareness of the flux evident at this time in nanotechnology vocabulary, the American National Standards Institute has formed a Nanotechnology Standards Panel, which will address issues of standardizing nanotechnology nomenclature, a process that could take as long as two years.[13] Until then, the lack of standardized language will limit the effectiveness of searching nanotechnology resources (such as databases), requiring the searcher to creatively anticipate terms that appear in different disciplines and fields.

NOTES

1. OED Online, 3rd ed., "Nanotechnology," 2006, at Dictionary.oed.com/cgi/entry/00320961 (accessed September 9, 2004).

2. National Institute for Occupational Safety and Health. *NIOSH, Nanotechnology, and Occupational Safety and Health Research—Frequently Asked Questions*, May 2005, at www.cdc.gov/niosh/topics/nanotech/faq.html (accessed July 14, 2006).

3. Richard P. Feynman, "There's Plenty of Room at the Bottom," *Engineering and Science* 23, no. 5 (February 1960): 22.

4. K. Eric Drexler, "Molecular Engineering: An Approach to the Development of General Capabilities for Molecular Manipulation," *Proceedings of the National Academy of Sciences* 78, no. 9 (September 1981): 5, 275–78.

5. K. Eric Drexler, *Engines of Creation: The Coming Era in Nanotechnology* (Garden City, NY: Doubleday, 1986).

6. National Science and Technology Council Interagency Working Group on NanoScience, Engineering and Technology, "Nanostructure Science and Technology: A Worldwide Study," August 1999, at www.ostp.gov/NSTC/html/iwgn/IWGN.Worldwide.Study/toc.htm (accessed September 30, 2004).

7. National Science and Technology Council. *National Nanotechnology Initiative: Research and Development Supporting the Next Industrial Revolution. Supplement to the President's FY 2004 Budget*, 2003, at www.nano.gov/html/res/fy04-pdf/fy04%20-%20small%20parts/NNI_FY04_D_intro.pdf (accessed July 14, 2006).

8. Joachim Schummer, "Multidisciplinarity, Interdisciplinarity, and Patterns of Research Collaboration in Nanoscience and Nanotechnology," *Scientometrics* 59, no. 3 (March-April 2004): 425–65.

9. Roger Cooper, "Nanotechnology: Small Beginnings with Great Potential," *Physics World* 2, no. 11 (November 1989): 60.

10. Mark Welland, "Editorial," *Nanotechnology* 13, (February 2002), www.iop.org/EJ/abstract/0957-4484/13/1/001.

11. The search statement "nano* not (nano2 or nano3 or nanomolar or nanosecond* or nanogram* or nanometer or nanometre)" was used as a topic keyword search.

12. Rick Weiss, "Language of Science Lags Behind Nanotech," *Washington Post*, May 17, 2004, final edition, 07(A), www.lexis-nexis.com/universe/.

13. Weiss, "Language of Science Lags Behind Nanotech," 07(A).

6

Atmospheric Chemistry

Meris Mandernach

Although planets throughout our solar system have undeniably interesting chemical dynamics, typical discussions of atmospheric chemistry deal with the chemistry of Earth's atmosphere. Earth's atmosphere is in a constant state of flux. Current atmospheric conditions are a far cry from those of the early atmosphere, which was composed mainly of methane and ammonia. Atmospheric chemistry has played an integral role in the history of life on this planet. The rise of atmospheric oxygen around 500 million years ago allowed a protective coat, the ozone layer, to form in the stratosphere and limit the amount of solar ultraviolet radiation that reaches the Earth. The fact that water exists above the freezing point, because of the prevalence of greenhouse gases in the atmosphere, allowed life to flourish on this planet. This chapter will focus on the information resources at the disposal of a researcher interested in delving into the field of atmospheric chemistry.

HISTORY AND DEVELOPMENT

Atmospheric chemistry is an amalgamation of other disciplines. It blurs disciplinary boundaries because researchers in this field must collaborate with geologists, hydrologists, botanists, oceanographers, climatologists, and many others to gain a complete picture of the diverse, complex, and interconnected processes that occur above, on, and below Earth's surface.

Environmental chemistry was first studied in the early eighteenth century, when several chemists were successful at determining the presence of the major chemical components of the atmosphere. In the nineteenth and twentieth centuries, the focus in the environmental chemical world shifted to the identification of trace gases, those present in less than one part per million, such as ozone. The source of these trace constituents can be found in geological, biological, and chemical processes.[1] Anthropogenic processes—chemical or biological emissions that are derived from human activities or influences—are also a factor.

Atmospheric chemistry evolved from the parent disciplines of chemistry and geology. As recently as 1960, very little was known about the chemistry of the atmosphere; however, through the rocket and satellite programs of the 1960s, scientists were able to explore the atmosphere of Earth as well as other planetary atmospheres in more depth and with more accuracy.

CHEMISTRY OF THE ATMOSPHERE

The atmosphere is made up of layers, described by specific altitude-temperature gradients. Starting at the surface of the Earth, the various layers include the troposphere (10–15 kilometers in altitude), the stratosphere (45–55 kilometers in altitude), the mesosphere (80–90 kilometers in altitude), the thermosphere (95–500 kilometers in altitude), and the exosphere (>500 kilometers in altitude). The lower four layers have specific boundaries, which are the tropopause, the stratopause, and the mesopause, respectively. As air moves vertically, the temperature varies based on the local pressure and water content.[2]

If water vapor is ignored, roughly 99.9 percent of the Earth's atmosphere is composed of nitrogen, oxygen, and argon. Chemical interactions among these elements cause atmospheric problems, such as smog, acid rain, and ozone holes, that attempt to disrupt the balance of life on Earth and potentially cause drastic climate change. The primary gases that influence these disruptions are carbon dioxide, methane, chlorofluorocarbons, nitrous oxide, and ozone. These gases are typically referred to as greenhouse gases, because they act as atmospheric thermal insulators. At the levels that exist naturally in the environment, these gases play a crucial role in protecting life at the surface of the Earth. They absorb solar radiation and, in turn, trap this heat in a gaseous envelope that maintains the temperature on Earth's surface.[3]

Over the past century, humans have been altering this delicate balance with biomass burnings, fossil fuel combustion, industrial gases, and intensive agriculture.[4] Anthropogenic emissions are the main cause for the abundance of trace species in the current atmosphere. With the appearance of the Antarctic ozone hole, the general public became aware of the impact that humans were having on the environment. Due to the fact that humans have drastically influenced the environment, many professional societies are focused on advocating for additional governmental legislation in this field.

The three main professional societies that support research in atmospheric chemistry include the American Meteorological Society, the American Geophysical Union, and the American Chemical Society. Each of these organizations has committees or divisions that specialize in issues pertinent to atmospheric chemistry. One critical issue the committees and divisions are examining is global climate change, specifically by monitoring ozone layers, aerosol levels, and the effects of anthropogenic emissions. The goal of this research is to influence policy that dictates environmental standards in the United States and around the globe.[5]

INFORMATION FLOW IN ATMOSPHERIC CHEMISTRY

The general flow of information in this field is similar to that of the parent disciplines. New data and experimental advances are initially reported through technical reports, in white papers, or on governmental websites. The first type of formally published literature, primary literature, consists of conference proceedings or journal articles. Second and tertiary literature, in the form of article indexes and books, are also prevalent in this field; however, the predominant avenue for information dispersal continues to be journal articles.

The first specialized journal in the field of atmospheric chemistry, *Journal of the Atmospheric Sciences*, appeared in 1962 and was published by the American Meteorological Society. The journal published quantitative research related to chemistry, physics, and dynamics of the atmosphere on Earth and other planets.

Another early journal that appeared in the field was *Atmospheric Environment: An International Journal*. This journal premiered in 1967. The focus of the journal is on studies in the areas of air pollution research and its applications, air quality and its effects, dispersion and transport, deposition, biosphere-atmosphere gas exchange, global atmospheric chemistry, radiation, and climate. Several other journals are standard sources for locating information on atmospheric chemistry topics, including *Journal of Geophysical Research-Atmospheres*, *Atmospheric Chemistry and Physics*, *Geophysical Research Letters*, *Environmental Science and Technology*, and *Journal of Atmospheric Chemistry*.

Presentations at conferences also contribute to the body of literature in environmental and atmospheric research. Conferences that hold sessions related to atmospheric chemistry include Environmental Physics Conference; International Conference on Climate Change and Ozone Protection; International Conference on Modeling, Monitoring and Management of Air Pollution; American Meteorological Society Annual Meeting; and the American Chemical Society National Meeting. Complete presentations or abstracts from these conferences may be added to the literature in print or online in the form of conference proceedings.

Additionally, much of the atmospheric data is collected by equipment purchased through grants that are funded by the U.S. federal government. Therefore, government reports are a valuable resource in this field. Many of these government-affiliated programs distribute information via their Internet websites. Some of this information can be found as preprints at government or academic websites.

Several U.S. government agencies dispense information about the topic of atmospheric chemistry. The National Oceanic and Atmospheric Agency (NOAA) gathers information regarding oceans, atmosphere, space, and the sun. NOAA, which falls under the Department of Commerce, was established in 1970.[6] NOAA supports many research opportunities through grants and research programs in the area of atmospheric chemistry. One recently established program is the Atmospheric Composition and Climate Program, which examines ozone depletion and climate change and monitors air quality.[7]

The National Aeronautics and Space Administration (NASA) studies the Earth's atmosphere with a research focus on the Earth's radiation balance and climate, atmospheric chemistry, and data management. Researchers use field experiments and study information gathered by aircraft, balloons, ground instruments, and Earth-orbiting satellites. All information obtained from the NASA satellites, including data on radiation, clouds, aerosols, and tropospheric chemistry, is freely available through the Atmospheric Sciences Data Center.[8]

The U.S. Environmental Protection Agency (EPA) has many valuable resources for researchers interested in atmospheric chemistry. The EPA distributes information on radiation, air pollution, radioactive materials, fuel economy, acid rain, climate protection, the ozone layer, and urban air quality.[9]

The mission of the U.S. Department of Energy (DOE) focuses on four strategic goals, one of which is the environment.[10] The Carbon Dioxide Information Analysis Center is the primary source of data on global change and the information analysis center of the DOE. The center has a searchable database that covers the topics of concentrations of carbon dioxide and other radioactive gases in the atmosphere, the role of the terrestrial biosphere and the oceans in the biogeochemical cycles of greenhouse gases, long-term climate trends, the effects of elevated carbon dioxide on vegetation, and the vulnerability of coastal areas to rising sea level.[11]

Organizations that determine environmental policy for the United States or other countries are another source of potentially useful information. In 1988, the Intergovernmental Panel on Climate Change (IPCC) was established to address viable options about the problem of global climate change. Although it does not conduct or sponsor research, the role of the

IPCC is to "assess on a comprehensive, objective, open and transparent basis the scientific, technical and socio-economic information relevant to understanding the scientific basis of risk of human-induced climate change, its potential impacts, and options for adaptation and mitigation."[12]

Another key player in advocating for legislation in the field of atmospheric chemistry is the National Academies. The National Academies comprise four organizations: the National Academy of Sciences, the National Academy of Engineering, the Institute of Medicine, and the National Research Council. The National Academies carry out "a wide range of activities on issues related to global-scale climate changes, land use and land cover, oceans and freshwater resources, atmospheric chemistry, and ecological systems resulting from natural variability or human influences, and the potential impacts of these changes on human systems and ecosystems."[13]

ATMOSPHERIC CHEMISTRY AND THE LIBRARY

Although atmospheric chemistry concerns have been prevalent since the early 1800s at various locations around the world, it did not officially become a distinct field until 1975. In April of that year, atmospheric chemistry was added as an official subject heading in the Library of Congress classification system.[14] Until that time, researchers had to seek out information by examining the parent disciplines of chemistry and geology.

As journal articles compose the majority of literature in the sciences, it is important to become familiar with database resources that cover this field. Atmospheric chemistry journals are included in a variety of subject databases, because the field is dependant on the literature of many other disciplines. Most of the relevant information about atmospheric chemistry can be found in the databases of the parent fields.

SUBSCRIPTION DATABASE RESOURCES

SciFinder Scholar, an American Chemical Society database, is the premier index for all chemically related searches and is international in scope. The database is composed of *Chemical Abstracts Plus* (bibliographic database), the *CAS Registry* file (substance database), *CHEMCATS* (chemical catalogs online), *CHEMLIST* (regulated chemicals), *CASREACT* (reactions), and *MEDLINE* (the National Library of Medicine's bibliographic database, the electronic version of *Index Medicus* in all its forms). *Chemical Abstracts Plus* includes references to articles, patents, conferences, books, and dissertations and covers the time period from 1907 to 2005. *MEDLINE* has complete coverage in *SciFinder Scholar* from 1957 to 2005.

The *Meteorological and Geoastrophysical Abstracts* covers literature world-wide on meteorology, climatology, atmospheric chemistry and physics, as-trophysics, physical oceanography, hydrology, glaciology, and related envi-ronmental sciences. The content, composed of citations to journal articles, conference proceedings, books, and technical reports, is updated monthly and covers the literature from 1974 to 2005.

Science Citation Index is a multidisciplinary database of nearly 4,000 core science and technical journals that span over 100 disciplines. A researcher is able to administer a broad, comprehensive search through the journal lit-erature, searching by keyword, author, or cited author. With the cited author search, a user is able to search forward or backward through the literature. This database is particularly useful in interdisciplinary fields, because it al-lows one to cross disciplinary boundaries and search in many subject-specific databases simultaneously.

The *Inspec* database covers literature in the fields of physics, astronomy and astrophysics, optics and optoelectronics, electrical engineering, elec-tronics, and computers and computing technology. The database is based on three *Science Abstracts Journals* print publications: *Physics Abstracts, Com-puter and Control Abstracts*, and *Electrical and Electronics Abstracts*. This bibli-ographic database includes many sources of information in the physics sub-file related to the topics of atmospheric sciences and climatology and meteorology. This database is particularly useful for searching early publi-cations in the fields of astronomy, astrophysics, or environmental science. One of the best features of *Inspec* is its extensive controlled vocabulary the-saurus. This database is updated weekly and primarily covers journal arti-cles but also contains references to conference proceedings, books, reports, dissertations, and patents from 1969 to 2005.

GeoRef, established in 1966 by the American Geological Institute, pro-vides access to worldwide literature in the fields of geology and geophysics. It is a good source for information on several aspects of atmospheric chem-istry, including global climate change and global warming. This database provides access to over 2.3 million references to articles, books, maps, con-ference papers, reports, and theses from 1785 to 2005 for the United States and from 1933 to 2005 for the rest of the world.

FREE DATABASE RESOURCES

The EPA tracks current topics of interest via the Airlinks web page at www.epa.gov/airlinks. The information and links to Internet resources change on a monthly basis. This is an excellent resource for those new to the field who need to locate background information. However, it also proves useful to any researcher in the field who needs to stay abreast of the EPA's polices with regards to chemistry of the atmosphere.

Preprints, as defined by the U.S. Department of Energy Office of Scientific and Technical Information, are "documents in pre-publication status, particularly an article submitted to a journal for publication."[15] Many agencies have established preprint servers related to the field of atmospheric chemistry: Los Alamos National Laboratory's E-print archive at http://lanl.arxiv.org/, the U.S. Department of Energy's E-print Network at www.osti.gov/eprints, a chemistry E-print server at www.sciencedirect.com/preprintarchive, Scientific Electronic Library Online at www.scielo.org, and PubMedCentral at www.pubmedcentral.nih.gov.

The most important method for searching the literature, as in any good literature search, is to use pearl-growing techniques.[16] Pearl growing is the process of finding a reference on a research topic and then using the information found in that reference, such as subject headings or keywords, to plan another search that provides more precise results. Brainstorming additional terms allows the researcher to cast the broadest net and improve the retrieval of relevant records. Therefore, although there are several databases that include the term "atmospheric chemistry," it may be useful to search similar subjects including chemistry of the atmosphere, environmental chemistry and climate change, air pollution, aerosol particles, climatology, air chemistry, air-sea interaction, industrial hygiene, environmental transport, climate, photolysis, stratosphere, air analysis, environmental pollution, dust particles, or clouds.

To find literature before 1975, when atmospheric chemistry was added to indexes as an official subject heading, the best approach is to search where climate and chemistry overlap in the literature. Atmospheric chemistry was initially examined in relation to impact from plants, sulfur emissions, radioactive fallout, or specific geographic regions of the world. Therefore, look for the following search terms: fertilizers, coal, atmosphere, pollution, lasers, radio waves, and radioactive substances.

An effective method for finding relevant information is by properly structuring a search based on the organization of the subject literature, mining the appropriate sources, and using appropriate search terms. Using these strategies, scientists will be ready to embark on research in this interdisciplinary field.

NOTES

1. Barbara J. Finlayson-Pitts and James N. Pitts Jr., *Atmospheric Chemistry: Fundamentals and Experimental Techniques* (New York: Wiley, 1986), 3–10.

2. John H. Seinfeld and Spyros N. Pandis, *Atmospheric Chemistry and Physics: From Air Pollution to Climate Change* (New York: Wiley. 1998), 2–9.

3. D. L. Albritton, "Atmospheric Chemistry and Global Change: The Scientist's Viewpoint," in *The Chemistry of the Atmosphere: Its Impact on Global Change*, ed. Jack G. Calvert (Oxford: Blackwell Scientific Publications, 1994), 3.

4. Donald J. Wuebbles, Guy P. Brasseur, and Henning Rodhe, "Changes in the Chemical Composition of the Atmosphere and Potential Impacts," in *Atmospheric Chemistry in a Changing World: An Integration and Synthesis of a Decade of Tropospheric Chemistry Research*, ed. Guy P. Brasseur, Ronald G. Prinn, and Alexander A. P. Pszenny (Berlin: Springer-Verlag, 2003), 1–13.

5. "American Geophysical Union," July 3, 2006, at www.agu.org (accessed August 24, 2004).

6. "The National Oceanic and Atmospheric Agency," July 7, 2006, at www.noaa.gov (accessed August 24, 2004).

7. "Climate Monitoring and Diagnostics Laboratory," October 1, 2005, at www.cmdl.noaa.gov/index.php (accessed August 21, 2004).

8. "NASA Langley Atmospheric Sciences Data Center," June 26, 2006, at eosweb.larc.nasa.gov (accessed August 23, 2004).

9. "Office of Air and Radiation, U.S. Environmental Protection Agency," June 26, 2006, at www.epa.gov/oar (accessed August 24, 2004).

10. "U.S. Department of Energy," at www.energy.gov/engine/content.do?BT_CODE=ABOUTDOE (accessed September 1, 2004).

11. "Carbon Dioxide Information Analysis Center," April 21, 2006, at cdiac.esd.ornl.gov (accessed September 1, 2004).

12. "Intergovernmental Panel on Climate Change," May 31, 2006, at www.ipcc.ch (accessed September 21, 2004).

13. "Global Change at the National Academies," 2006, at dels.nas.edu (accessed September 21, 2004).

14. Lynn M. El-Hoshy, e-mail message to author, September 16, 2004.

15. Sharon M. Jordan, "Preprint Servers: Status, Challenges, and Opportunities of the New Digital Publishing Paradigm," *InForum '99*, May 25, 1999, at www.osti.gov/inforum99/papers/jordan.html (accessed September 25 2004).

16. Donald T. Hawkins and Robert Wagers, "Online Bibliographic Search Strategy Development," *Online* 6, no. 3 (May 1982): 12–19.

7

Bioethics

Steven Baumgart and Carla H. Lee

HISTORY AND DEVELOPMENT

The *Oxford English Dictionary* defines bioethics as "the discipline dealing with ethical questions that arise as a result of advances in medicine and biology."[1] While this practical definition works well, it masks the true number of disciplines that may have an interest in bioethics. This is a truly interdisciplinary subject, bringing together such diverse disciplines as medicine, biology, theology, philosophy, and law. Paralleling the epistemological methods in the disciplines involved, authors in Bioethics tend to be reflective in nature. Therefore, they are continually working towards a fuller definition and understanding of the origins of their field, and consequently many historical accounts have been written. This chapter gives a brief summary of the formation of the field, but readers particularly interested in the history of bioethics should read Albert R. Jonsen's book, *Birth of Bioethics*, M. L. Tina Stevens' *Bioethics in America*, and the article "The History of Bioethics: An Essay Review" by Robert Martensen. The *Cambridge Quarterly of Health Care Ethics* published an issue in 2002 that contained several personal historical accounts from people who had been working in the discipline in the early 1970s. *The Source Book in Bioethics: A Documentary History*, is an excellent source for those who would like to see the text of the policies, legal acts, and reports that led to the formation of the field.

The term "bioethics" was coined twice in the early 1970s,[2] each use describing two different ideas. Van Rensselaer Potter used the term "bioethics" in 1971 in his book *Bioethics: Bridge to the Future*, as a term to describe a discipline that would achieve "the new wisdom that is so desperately needed: biological knowledge and human values."[3] Also in 1971, R. Sergeant

Shriver, the first director of the Peace Corps, used the term "bioethics" in a discussion with Andre Hellegers, the founder and first director of the Kennedy Institute of Ethics, as they were developing plans for a center devoted to the study of philosophical and ethical problems in biomedicine at Georgetown University. While Potter used the term to refer to all aspects of biology in relation to ethics and society, Shriver focused on the medical field. The latter interpretation of the term has become the dominant use, sometimes being used interchangeably with medical ethics. However, there is a difference between bioethics and medical ethics. Bioethics expands upon medical ethics by including other disparate disciplines and moving ethical discussions away from doctor/patient relationships and towards medicine/society discussions. In degrees, bioethics is a more socially applied field, and medical ethics is more individualistic.

While the word may have been coined in the early 1970s, the roots of bioethics stretch much further back. Prior to the Industrial Revolution, medicine was practiced as a "cottage industry."[4] There were no professionally defined ethical standards, but professional ethics were necessarily equated with personal character, and each doctor was expected to behave in an ethical and moral manner as an individual. In 1847, the American Medical Association introduced their Code of Ethics, which began the codification of medical ethics.

The state of medical ethics continued in much the same way until after World War II, when the horrors perpetrated by the Nazi doctors and the overwhelming power of the nuclear bomb combined to cause many to question whether scientific progress should continue unchecked. It became the first major paradigm shift in medical ethics from an individualistic approach to social concerns and marks the beginning of the transition from medical ethics to bioethics. Another event that coalesced the transformation of medical ethics into bioethics occurred in 1962, when a Seattle hospital created a committee to decide who should receive life-saving access to the newly invented dialysis machines. This was one of the first committees charged with making these types of decisions that consisted primarily of laypeople instead of medical practitioners.[5] Then, in 1972, the revelations of the Tuskegee study, in which African-American males were left untreated for syphilis in order to monitor and study the progression of the disease, introduced further questions regarding the ability of medical professionals to reliably regulate their own research involving human subjects.[6] These questions led to extensive discussions that ultimately resulted in the creation of institutional review boards at research and educational facilities. These boards are run independently from disciplines and departments, and are charged with reviewing the ethics of research involving human subjects. They are a further indicator of the transformation of medical ethics' isolation into a more society-oriented field of bioethics.

Crucial to the development of bioethics as a field was the development of two research centers. Prior to their establishment, the primary work of bioethics was being conducted at conferences. These centers "gave permanent homes to the discourse of bioethical concern."[7] The Hastings Center, incorporated in 1969, and the Kennedy Institute of Ethics, in 1971, created the first settings for the study of ethical problems in medicine by theologians, philosophers, and doctors. Both leaders in the formation of the field, these two centers contributed to the development of bioethics in different ways. The Hastings Center "fostered interdisciplinary discourse by arranging working groups and task forces."[8] The center also produced the first journal in the field, the *Hastings Center Report*, beginning in 1971. The Kennedy Institute took a more academic approach, "providing professorships, fellowships and courses."[9] The institute also had a profound and continued effect on the bioethics literature by publishing the *Bibliography of Bioethics*, and *The Encyclopedia of Bioethics* and by establishing the National Reference Center for Bioethics Literature. The Hastings Center, the Kennedy Institute of Ethics, and their publications continue to be preeminent today, although the literature in bioethics-specific publications and the inclusion of bioethics-related topics in journals of a variety of disciplines have grown.

SEARCHING FOR BIOETHICS LITERATURE

Background Information

To learn more about a specific topic in bioethics, its history, and current state, the *Encyclopedia of Bioethics* is an important source. This five-volume work includes detailed articles on many topics, and its appendices also includes compilations of the various codes and oaths of ethics that have been developed, as well as many of the legal codes that may be of interest. For example, the first article in the encyclopedia is "Abortion."[10] This weighty topic is given forty-two pages, which includes a discussion of the general ethical and legal aspects of abortion, and then also considers the religious aspects in the Jewish, Roman Catholic, Protestant, and Islamic faiths. There are excellent bibliographies that provide access to key works (mostly secondary), to pursue the topic in more depth. In addition to being one of the most respected reference works in the field, the first edition of this set, produced by the Kennedy Institute of Ethics, defined the field.[11] In the most recent edition, the new editor notes that the first edition was "immediately acknowledged as a landmark reference defining the field."[12]

For further information regarding the structure of the current literature and how to search for it, the single best article, written by the Kennedy Institute of Ethics, that describes searching for materials is "After Bioethics-line: Online Searching of the Bioethics Literature."[13] Also notable is the

FAQ from the National Library of Medicine entitled "Question: How Do I Identify Older Medical Journal Articles?"[14] Finally, H. Fangerau, in "Finding European Bioethical Literature: An Evaluation of the Leading Abstracting and Indexing Services," provides an eye-opening discussion regarding the interdisciplinary nature of bioethics searching and how searching a single source is not sufficient.[15]

Selecting Search Terms

Finding the right subject terms to search can be part of the challenge in finding bioethics materials. Most indexes provide a system of controlled vocabulary often known as subject headings. These terms are the official vocabulary used to communicate a concept or idea within a specific index. In *MEDLINE* and *PubMed*, this vocabulary is primarily derived from the National Library of Medicine's Medical Subject Headings (known as MeSH). *MEDLINE* is the National Library of Medicine's bibliographic database that covers the areas of medicine, nursing, dentistry, and veterinary medicine including ethics-related materials in those areas. *MEDLINE* is frequently a subscription-based resource and available at many libraries. *PubMed* is more inclusive, and it is publicly available. It includes *MEDLINE* as well as citations to articles from *OLDMEDLINE* (the index that preceded *MEDLINE* from 1950–1965) and in-process citations that have not yet been added to *MEDLINE*, but will be in the near future. The primary difference between *OLDMEDLINE* and *MEDLINE* is that the latter uses MeSH vocabulary, while the former did not use any form of controlled vocabulary. For both *OLDMEDLINE* and in-process citations, MeSH vocabulary terms have not yet been assigned to the citation, but there is currently an effort to add MeSH vocabulary to *OLDMEDLINE* citations.

Before searching *MEDLINE* or *PubMed*, determine the relevant MeSH vocabulary terms for which to search. MeSH terms are compiled in an independently searchable database entitled *MeSH Database*.[16] It is available publicly from the National Library of Medicine. A keyword search in the *MeSH Database* will retrieve relevant subject headings that can be used in *MEDLINE* or *PubMed*. Be sure to examine a term's full record to see related terms, broader terms, and narrower terms that can be used for further searching in the *MeSH Database* itself as well as within *MEDLINE* or *PubMed*.

However, for topics that are currently emerging, there are rarely corresponding subject headings or controlled vocabulary terms. It takes time to institutionalize the vocabulary and codify it within the *MeSH Database*, and therefore for the most current topics, keyword searches are still necessary. Searches in the *MeSH Database* alone may not lead to adequate search terms in a new research area. Therefore, keyword searches directly in an index such as *MEDLINE* or *PubMed* is advisable. Even if subject headings exist, it is suitable to conduct a keyword search to be thorough, since subject terms are not commonly applied retrospectively.

In general, there are several types of documents to search for when in pursuit of bioethics literature, including journal articles, monographic materials, books, book chapters, audiovisual materials, and Internet websites. Following are some general strategies for finding different types of materials on bioethics.

Searching for Journal Articles

The mechanics for finding materials related to bioethics is significantly dependent upon its history as a field. As previously discussed, even before "bioethics" became part of the English vernacular in 1970, the fundamental ideas composing the discipline were present in academic and scholarly circles. Prior to 1970, bioethics was discussed in terms of medical ethics on a socio-political scale. By 1974, the term "bioethics" could be searched as both a keyword and as a subject heading in most indexes.[17] In 1979, the index *BIOETHICSLINE* was produced by the Kennedy Institute of Ethics as part of the National Library of Medicine's growing assortment of specialized online databases. Parts of *BIOETHICSLINE* were subsequently integrated into *MEDLINE*, *PubMed*, and *LocatorPlus* in 2000 as part of the National Library of Medicine's effort to consolidate its specialized databases.[18] Journal citations are now indexed in *MEDLINE* and *PubMed*. The records for books, on the other hand, have been integrated into *LocatorPlus*, the online catalog for the National Library of Medicine's collection. Prior to the consolidation, *BIOETHICSLINE* had only indexed those books that were owned by the National Library of Medicine. The additions to *LocatorPlus* were solely fuller records that included abstracts and more complete MeSH subject headings. The complexity of this history dictates that searching strategies need to be adapted to the time period for which one wants to search. In bioethics, the key date to remember when searching is 1952.

Pre-1952

Prior to 1952, it is necessary to consult print indexes to find bioethics materials because no central databases covered bioethics before that date. As with most print indexes, cross-referencing of citations is unlikely, so it is essential that one searches for the terms "ethics, medical" as well as related or more specific terms to be sure one does not miss items. One print index used for medical literature prior to 1952 is the *Index Medicus*, published from 1879 to 1926, which contains information on journals, books, and pamphlets. It is intended to be a supplement for the *Index-Catalogue of the Library of the Surgeon-General's Office*, published from 1880 to 1961, which also contains references to journals and books. Some materials contained in one index are not covered in the other.

From 1916 through 1926, one will find a further index source for medical literature in the *Quarterly Cumulative Index to Current Literature* by the American Medical Association. From 1927 through 1956, the *Index Medicus* became the *Quarterly Cumulative Index Medicus*. As a final supplement, from 1941 to 1959, consult the *Current List of Medical Literature*, published by the Army Medical Library and the Armed Forces Medical Library. It covers some journals not contained within the *Index Medicus*.[19]

While seemingly complicated, this list can be boiled down to two main sources: the *Index Medicus* in all its forms, and the *Index-Catalog of the Library of the Surgeon-General's Office*. Neither source is comprehensive on its own. Used in combination, they are likely to be more complete. However, they will inevitably fail to provide alternative viewpoints outside of the field of medicine. That means that even if discussions related to bioethics existed prior to 1952, these publications will be difficult to find. Besides searching *Index Medicus* and the *Index-Catalog*, refer to other print indexes outside of the medical discipline. A few other print sources for searching outside the field of medicine are *Cumulative Index to Nursing and Allied Health Literature*, *The Philosopher's Index*, *ATLA Religion Index*, *Psychological Abstracts*, *Social Work Abstracts*, and *Index to Legal Periodicals and Books*. Their titles reflect the disciplines that they cover. None are comprehensive, and as with other print sources, it is necessary to search them using multiple approaches and multiple search terms to be consistently successful.

For basic search strategies for bioethics, there are essentially two methodologies. Since the term "bioethics" did not become part of the English language until 1970, it is impossible to find materials using that term. Instead, try using the preceding terms "medical ethics" or "ethics, medical." However, this approach will only yield results that are related to broader ethical issues, and results will vary greatly depending on which topics the materials are focused. To narrow down a search, look for specific topics within the relevant indexes.

For example, to find materials related to euthanasia prior to 1952, one should begin by examining the *Index Medicus* and exploring the index for topics related to euthanasia. In the *Index Medicus*, MeSHs work well, so in order to find terms for euthanasia, one should explore the *MeSH Database*. In the case of euthanasia, a related subject heading is "suicide, assisted." To achieve a comprehensive search, one should look for specific topics (euthanasia and suicide, assisted) as well as broad terms (medical ethics). This process must be repeated for each index relevant to the topic outside of *Index Medicus* and the *Index-Catalog*.

Post-1952

In 1979, the online index *BIOETHICSLINE* debuted. Compiled by the Kennedy Institute of Ethics, it became the primary source to find bioethics literature. Its creation corresponded with the emergence of the new MeSH term "bioethics" in 1978 and signaled the dawning of an easier, more centralized index for bioethics. For several decades, it was a separate online database, but in 2000, it became integrated into *MEDLINE*. The year 1952 is the beginning date for materials entered into the *OLDMEDLINE*. As mentioned earlier, *OLDMEDLINE* is the online predecessor to the current *MEDLINE*. Its primary distinction from *MEDLINE* is its lack of controlled vocabulary and abstracts. Therefore, 1952 is the date of sources for which one can search using online indexes. *OLDMEDLINE* is not contained within *MEDLINE*, and therefore, searching only *MEDLINE* limits the dates of coverage from 1966 to 2005. For that reason, the most efficient mechanism by which to search is *PubMed* (pubmed.gov) because it contains both *OLDMEDLINE* and *MEDLINE*.[20]

Performing a comprehensive search on an interdisciplinary topic is more difficult because no database is complete in its coverage of any discipline. This problem is even more pronounced in bioethics, because so many disciplines may publish articles of interest. Its connections to philosophy, religion, law, social work, and psychology necessitate the exploration of materials related to bioethics in the databases for those disciplines as well. Searching *PubMed* and *MEDLINE* is not enough. Part of the post-1952 search strategy is to go beyond medical resources and conduct searches in other discipline-related databases and indexes.

In a study examining the coverage of European bioethics journals in thirty-six databases, including *MEDLINE*, it was determined that "A combined search in the top ten databases showing the highest coverage would only cover 42.5% of the journals in question."[21]

To increase the likelihood of achieving a more comprehensive search, conduct searches in such interdisciplinary sources as *Social Science Citation Index* and *Science Citation Index*. Researchers can start with a list of citations, a bibliography of their topic, or a list of experts in the field. Search for each citation or person to determine other articles that may have cited those articles to find additional useful literature. In this way, the searcher's bibliography is likely to expand in unforeseen interdisciplinary directions based on the wider impact of the original article.

Searching For Books

Up to this point, the discussion has been limited to journal literature in bioethics and has not addressed the differentiation that exists with books and book chapters. Some book chapters and books will be discovered using the same methods used to find journal articles. However, there are some specific techniques that can be employed to locate books. As with journal articles, the history of bioethics determines the method that should be used. As mentioned earlier, in 1978, the National Library of Medicine codified "bioethics" as part of its official vocabulary by making it into a MeSH term, but it was being used as early as 1974. To further complicate this timeline, in 2000, *BIOETHICSLINE* was integrated into *MEDLINE*. Previous to that integration, *BIOETHICSLINE* covered articles, books, and book chapters. However, as part of the integration, the National Library of Medicine separated *BIOETHICSLINE* into its component parts, and books and book chapters were incorporated into *LocatorPlus*, the National Library of Medicine's monographic catalog, instead of *MEDLINE*.[22]

For books alone, the primary index used is *WorldCat*, a consolidated catalog of thousands of libraries. The key date to remember for finding books in *WorldCat* is 1974. Materials before 1974 related to Bioethics will be indexed using the subject headings "ethics, medical" or "medical ethics." After and including 1974, materials can be found using the subject heading "bioethics," but the terms "ethics, medical" and "medical ethics" continue to be used. Therefore, it is best to use all terms regardless of date, as well as to conduct keyword searches using "bioethics" and other topic-specific terms. However, *WorldCat* does not contain book chapters, so it is better to use *LocatorPlus* to find those.

In addition to *LocatorPlus*, searches for book chapters related to bioethics will vary considerably depending on the capabilities and coverage of the complementary indexes such as *Philosopher's Index*, *ATLA*, and so on. It is recommended to explore these other sources in order to include specialty viewpoints.

Internet Websites

Since bioethics is dependent on societies and ethics centers for its sustained footprint, these societies' and centers' websites become an excellent directory of credible information available on the Internet. The two most notable societies and centers are:

- The Hastings Center (www.thehastingscenter.org) and
- The Kennedy Institute of Ethics (www.georgetown.edu/research/kie/site/index.htm).

Visit these websites first and use them as a gateway to further information.

NOTES

1. *Oxford English Dictionary Online,* "Bioethics," 2006, at dictionary.oed.com/ (accessed May 16, 2005).

2. Warren Thomas Reich, "The Word 'Bioethics': Its Birth and the Legacies of those Who Shaped It," *Kennedy Institute of Ethics Journal* 4, no. 4 (December 1994): 319–35.

3. Van Rensselaer Potter, *Bioethics: Bridge to the Future* (Englewood Cliff, NJ: Prentice-Hall, 1971), 2.

4. Erich H. Loewy, "Bioethics: Past, Present, and an Open Future," *Cambridge Quarterly of Healthcare Ethics* 11, no. 4 (October 2002): 388–97.

5. Albert R. Jonsen, *The Birth of Bioethics* (New York: Oxford University Press, 1998): 211–14.

6. Jonsen, *The Birth of Bioethics,* 146–48.

7. Jonsen, *The Birth of Bioethics,* 20.

8. Jonsen, *The Birth of Bioethics,* 24.

9. Jonsen, *The Birth of Bioethics,* 24.

10. Stephen G. Post, ed., *Encyclopedia of Bioethics,* 3rd ed. (New York: Macmillan Reference, 2004): 1–42.

11. Warren Thomas Reich, "Shaping and Mirroring the Field: The Encyclopedia of Bioethics," *The Story of Bioethics: From Seminal Works to Contemporary Explorations,* ed. Jennifer K. Walter (Washington, D.C.: Georgetown University Press, 2003), 165–96.

12. Post, *Encyclopedia of Bioethics,* vii.

13. "After Bioethicsline: Online Searching of the Bioethics Literature," *Kennedy Institute of Ethics Journal* 11, no. 4 (December 2001): 387–90.

14. National Library of Medicine, "Question: How Do I Identify Older Medical Journal Articles?" *FAQ: Index Medicus Chronology,* December 2004, at www.nlm.nih .gov/services/indexmedicus.html (accessed October 4, 2004).

15. H. Fangerau, "Finding European Bioethical Literature: An Evaluation of the Leading Abstracting and Indexing Services," *Journal of Medical Ethics* 30, no. 3 (June 2004): 299–303.

16. National Library of Medicine, "Medical Subject Headings—Homepage," April 10, 2006, at www.nlm.nih.gov/mesh/meshhome.html (accessed October 17, 2004).

17. Reich, "The Word 'Bioethics'": Its Birth and the Legacies of Those Who Shaped It," 330.

18. "After Bioethicsline: Online Searching of the Bioethics Literature," 387–89.

19. National Library of Medicine, "Question: How Do I Identify Older Medical Journal Articles?"

20. National Library of Medicine, "*OLDMEDLINE,*" June 7, 2006, at www.nlm .nih.gov/databases/databases_oldmedline.html (accessed October 10, 2004).

21. Fangerau, "Finding European Bioethical Literature: An Evaluation of the Leading Abstracting and Indexing Services," 299–303.

22. "After Bioethicsline: Online Searching of the Bioethics Literature," 387.

BIBLIOGRAPHY

"After Bioethicsline: Online Searching of the Bioethics Literature." *Kennedy Institute of Ethics Journal* 11, no. 4 (December 2001): 387–90.

American Society for Bioethics and Humanities (ASBH). www.asbh.org (11 October 2004).

Fangerau, H. "Finding European Bioethical Literature: An Evaluation of the Leading Abstracting and Indexing Services." *Journal of Medical Ethics* 30, no. 3 (June 2004): 299–303.

Hastings Center. www.thehastingscenter.org (11 October 2004).

Jonsen, Albert R. *The Birth of Bioethics*. New York: Oxford University Press, 1998.

Jonsen, Albert R., Robert M. Veatch & LeRoy Walters, eds. *Source Book in Bioethics: A Documentary History*. Washington, D.C.: Georgetown University Press, 1998.

Kennedy Institute of Ethics. www.georgetown.edu/research/kie/site/index.htm (11 October 2004).

Loewy, Erich H. "Bioethics: Past, Present, and an Open Future." *Cambridge Quarterly of Healthcare Ethics* 11, no. 4 (October 2002): 388–97.

Martensen, Robert. "The History of Bioethics: An Essay Review." *Journal of the History of Medicine* 56, no. 2 (April 2001): 168–75.

National Institutes of Health, Inter-Institute Bioethics Interest Group (BIG), and Office of Extramural Research (OER). www.nih.gov/sigs/bioethics (11 October 2004).

National Library of Medicine. *Medical Subject Headings—Homepage*. www.nlm.nih.gov/mesh/meshhome.html (17 October 2004).

National Library of Medicine, *MeSH Database*, www.ncbi.nlm.nih.gov/entrez/query.fcgi?db=mesh (17 October 2004).

National Library of Medicine, OLDMEDLINE. www.nlm.nih.gov/databases/databases_oldmedline.html (10 October 2004).

National Library of Medicine. "Question: How Do I Identify Older Medical Journal Articles." *FAQ: Index Medicus Chronology*. www.nlm.nih.gov/services/index medicus.html (4 October 2004).

Potter, Van Rensselaer. *Bioethics: Bridge to the Future*. Englewood Cliff, NJ: Prentice-Hall, 1971.

Reich, Warren Thomas. "The Word 'Bioethics': Its Birth and the Legacies of Those Who Shaped It." *Kennedy Institute of Ethics Journal* 4, no. 4 (December 1994): 319–35.

"Scope Note 38: Bioethics Resources on the Web," *Kennedy Institute of Ethics Journal* 10, no. 2 (June 2000): 175–88.

Stevens, M. L. Tina. *Bioethics in America: Origins and Cultural Politics*. Baltimore, MD: Johns Hopkins University Press, 2000.

University of Minnesota, Center for Bioethics. www.med.umn.edu/bioethics (11 October 2004).

University of Tübingen, Interdepartmental Center for Ethics in the Sciences and Humanities. www.uni-tuebingen.de/zew (11 October 2004).

8

Computational Biology

Kevin Messner

THE INFLUENCE OF THE GENOMIC REVOLUTION AND THE INTERNET

The 1990s marked the emergence of a revolution in the biological sciences. Beginning in the late 1980s and culminating in the year 2000, the Human Genome Project, arguably the first "big science" project in biology, mapped and sequenced the three billion nucleotide bases of DNA in human cells.[1] This enormous undertaking marked—and itself catalyzed—major changes in how biologists and health researchers approach their work.[2] For the first time, scientists have available a view of the entire scope of the molecular workings of our cells—all the genes and proteins that form our bodies. With the high-throughput sequencing and analysis technologies emerging from the Human Genome Project, hundreds of other organisms important to health, agriculture, and industry are now sequenced or are in progress. Scientists are able to perform complex experiments that simultaneously gather data on the operation of hundreds of genes, and functional and comparative analysis of genes and genomes is rapidly advancing.

Concurrent with these developments in biology and computer science, the Internet and World Wide Web emerged into wide public recognition and use. This coincidence was a fortunate one for biology, as the World Wide Web made the wide and rapid dissemination of data emerging from the Human Genome Project, and other publicly funded genomics endeavors, technically feasible and low in cost. Thus, much genome data has been placed online in public depositories, and scientists are able to view and use on demand the data and analyze and interpret it in the context of their own work.

The field of computational biology has emerged and gained considerable attention during this time, resulting in an abundance of published literature. It has become necessary to find increasingly sophisticated computational and statistical methods to efficiently store, manage, retrieve, process, analyze, and interpret the glut of DNA sequence and other biological data now available to researchers. Correspondingly, these are among the core goals of computational biology research and development.

DEFINING COMPUTATIONAL
BIOLOGY AND BIOINFORMATICS

An attempt to define the relationship between computational biology and bioinformatics may be instructive, if not definitive. There has been considerable debate as to what these terms (should) mean, and how they relate to each other.[3] Computational biology is typically considered to be a field broad in scope, while bioinformatics is regarded by some workers as a subset of computational biology. The Medical Subject Headings (MeSH) system is a widely used official thesaurus for medical and biological subject terms. MeSH defines computational biology as "a field of biology concerned with the development of techniques for the collection and manipulation of biological data, and the use of such data to make biological discoveries or predictions. This field encompasses all computational methods and theories applicable to molecular biology and areas of computer-based techniques for solving biological problems including manipulation of models and datasets."[4] Thus, computational biology potentially encompasses a wide variety of biological problems, including sequence analysis, computational modeling of biological structures and physiological functions, and even computational analysis of ecological problems.

The definitional problem and disagreement in usage emerges in deciding what aspects of computational biology are to be included in the term bioinformatics. Bioinformatics is sometimes defined very narrowly, but in other cases the term is given a much broader reach. In some narrow definitions, Bioinformatics relates only to the computational systems developed to manipulate biological sequence (DNA, RNA, protein) information. A *Dictionary of Biology* defines Bioinformatics as "The collection, storage, and analysis of DNA- and protein-sequence data using computerized systems."[5] In this sense, bioinformatics is limited to work on problems in sequence database maintenance and dynamic character string recognition, and computational biology is reserved for other types of biological data and computational problems. Most researchers, however, apply the term bioinformatics more loosely, to include (at least) computational systems dealing with analysis of many other types of molecular biological data sets, such as gene expression patterns, metabolic network models, and protein structure models. Knowledge management systems in biology, built for discovery of novel connections between known data objects (e.g., "data mining" of biological data), are also often referred to as bioinformatics tools, further broadening the scope of the term.[6] Finally, some researchers (as well as the MeSH system) consider computational biology and bioinformatics essentially as synonyms. For the purposes of this text, I will refer mainly to computational biology, as it can legitimately be considered the broader term, with the understanding that oftentimes the terms can be used interchangeably. In any case, the information sources and search strategies used by workers in the two fields are very similar.

HISTORY OF THE FIELD AND KEY ORGANIZATIONS

Though genome sequencing efforts and the World Wide Web in the 1990s did much to push forward the development of computational biology as a discrete field, the field has older roots. Computational biology may be considered to have begun in the development of biological sequence alignment algorithms used for the study of protein evolution in the 1960s. The Needleman–Wunsch[7] global alignment algorithm, published in 1970, and the Smith–Waterman[8] local alignment algorithm, published later in 1981, are particularly notable as classic computational biology tools. The 1970 paper may be reasonably (though somewhat arbitrarily) construed as marking the birth of computational biology as a distinct field.

MAKE-UP AND DEVELOPMENT OF THE COMPUTATIONAL BIOLOGY RESEARCH COMMUNITY

Computational biology has emerged as a distinct field from collaborations of workers in a variety of disciplines, including computer science, mathematics and statistics, biology, and medicine. The professional organizations and societies of these various disciplines have played important roles in propelling the field. The Institute of Electrical and Electronics Engineers (IEEE) and the Association for Computing Machinery (ACM) were active from the mid-1990s in sponsoring conferences and workshops devoted to computational biology. Established specialist organizations formed around neighboring fields, such as the American Medical Informatics Association. Medical informatics, which deals with the organization and use of information in health care, has also provided substantial publication and conferencing opportunities for computational biologists.

The International Society for Computational Biology (ISCB), created in 1997, has emerged as the principal membership organization for computational biology. This society originated from the meetings held at the Intelligent Systems in Molecular Biology (ISMB) conferences in the early 1990s. The ISMB meetings were among the first to actively bring together molecular biologists and computer scientists to discuss the potential of information technology to advance discovery in biology. The ISCB continues to hold the Intelligent Systems in Molecular Biology conference annually and sponsors some of the principal journals in computational biology and related fields. Other specialty organizations, such as Bioinformatics.org, have a significant online presence as providers of computational biology software and tools. A membership-based organization, Bioinformatics.org serves as a center for collaborative projects, emphasizing resource and tool development.

Leadership from government and the establishment of specialty government agencies have also been important to the growth of the field in the last decade. In the United States, the National Center for Biotechnology Information (NCBI)—a unit of the National Library of Medicine within the National Institutes of Health—was founded in 1988 and has played several key roles. First and foremost, NCBI took an early role as a storehouse and provider of biological sequence information with its sequence database *GenBank*. NCBI has also been an important developer of many analytical tools and services in the field.[9] Perhaps most famously, NCBI introduced in 1990 the BLAST sequence analysis algorithm.[10] BLAST is a program that allows researchers to detect similarities between two DNA or protein sequences. A much faster algorithm than many of its predecessors, BLAST allows researchers to use a particular sequence of interest to find other similar sequences in large databases such as *GenBank* (and potentially clues to the sequence's relationship or biological function). Most biomedical researchers are familiar with another NCBI development, *PubMed*, the popular website enabling searching of the *MEDLINE* biomedical literature database.

Aside from the National Center for Biotechnology Information in the United States, the European Bioinformatics Institute within European Molecular Biology Organization (EMBO, a multigovernmental agency) has been an important developer for a number of key computational biology databases and resources (e.g., the ensemble genome organization and annotation project). The tools developed at NCBI and EMBO have often served informally as touchstones for quality assessment of other experimental resources developed in computational biology. In addition to their internal research efforts, both NCBI and EMBO have been important financial supporters, organizers, and champions for scientists engaging in computational biology research.

STRUCTURE OF THE LITERATURE AND KEY SOURCES

A sampling of computational biology resources available on the Internet was reviewed in 2002.[11] Key sources of literature in this field and routes of access to that literature are discussed in this section with an explicit aim of guiding a new researcher in the field to some of the richest sources.

Journal and Conference Literature

Like most life and health sciences, the principal method for the dissemination of research literature in computational biology is the peer-reviewed journal article. The journal literature is used to announce new findings and establish priority for discovery. Review articles published in some journals do not typically announce new results but instead serve to summarize, assess, and synthesize past literature and the progress made in particular research problems at that moment in time.

While a number of specialty journals have been published at the interface of biology and mathematics as long ago as the 1960s, the most notable specialty title in computational biology was originally titled *Computer Applications in the Biosciences*. This title began publication in 1985 and emerged as a leading journal in the field after the journal's sponsoring organization, the International Society for Computational Biology, changed the journal's title to *Bioinformatics* in 1998. The journal publishes original research papers, "Applications Notes" (short write-ups on particular computational biology software applications and projects), as well as the annual Intelligent Systems in Molecular Biology conference proceedings.

The emerging "open access" scholarly publishing model is familiar and of interest to many involved in computational biology, as akin in spirit and principle to the "open source" code movement in the computer programming community. Much of the progress in computational biology research relies on the ability to link to and readily access the bulk of the biological literature to discover connections between seemingly unrelated research topics. Correspondingly, the International Society for Computational Biology has recently begun publication of *PLoS Computational Biology* as an open access journal title that deals with computational methods in biological research from the molecular to the ecological scales.

The journal *Nucleic Acids Research* also bears special mention. Since 1996, the January 1 issue of each year has been dedicated to reviews of public biological databases and repositories for computational biology research. The "database issue" has become an important current awareness source for developers and users of computational biology information sources (see the section "Biological Databases" below.) Similarly, each July 1 issue is dedicated to reviews of web-based computational biology analysis packages. Published by Oxford University Press, *Nucleic Acids Research* changed in 2005 from a subscription-based publication to an open access publication model.

Conference literature plays a small but relevant role in computational biology publication. As mentioned previously, IEEE and ACM have played important roles in providing a variety of topical conferences for researchers in the field, and consequently these societies' databases (*IEEE Xplore* and *ACM Digital Library*) contain a significant amount of relevant conference literature.

Access to the journal and conference literature is achieved most readily through research literature indexes (also known in their computerized forms as bibliographic databases). The following major indexes of interest to researchers in computational biology merit individual consideration: *MEDLINE, BIOSIS, SciFinder Scholar,* and *Inspec.*

MEDLINE

Produced by the National Library of Medicine, this database is the largest and most comprehensive bibliographic source for literature research in the health sciences. While the principal historical focus of *MEDLINE* is clinical medicine and medical research, a large number of basic science journals are indexed in the database, and it is heavily used by researchers in biochemistry, genetics, molecular biology, and other basic biological research areas. General and specialty journals dealing with computational biology are well represented in the database. Most records include the article abstract. *MEDLINE* is made freely available to the public online through the *PubMed* website (www.ncbi.nlm.nih.gov/entrez/query.fcgi?), although several other interfaces to *MEDLINE* are available either freely or commercially as licensed products. (In fact, the *MEDLINE* database is only one component of *PubMed*, and *PubMed* includes several sources of citations beyond those made available in *MEDLINE* itself.)[12] Because of the public availability and wide relevance of the contents of the *MEDLINE* database, it is a key model substrate used for research in alternative interfaces and automated textual data mining of biological literature.

As with all literature databases, the search interface can have a strong impact on the results. This is especially true in the case of a highly structured database with a sophisticated controlled vocabulary, such as is found in *MEDLINE*. The database uses the MeSH controlled vocabulary system. Bibliographic records added to *MEDLINE* are typically indexed under five to fifteen MeSH terms. In search interfaces, such as the *PubMed* website and Ovid *MEDLINE*, a thesaurus is used to help translate user queries into MeSH terminology and so connect user query to bibliographic citation.

The *PubMed* interface is designed to allow effective searching without strong knowledge of Boolean logic (AND, NOT, OR) or the use of MeSH (user queries are processed into MeSH terminology "behind the scenes"). Still, it is helpful to be familiar with some relevant subject terms to aid searching. One broad MeSH term frequently applied to this literature, "computational biology," has already been mentioned. A sampling of other MeSH terms of pertinence in this field includes: algorithms; computing methodologies; databases, genetic; databases, protein; gene expression profiling; genomics; mathematical computing; models, biological; models, genetics; protein interaction mapping; proteomics; sequence analysis; and systems biology. This list is far from exhaustive; however, the reader is recommended to further explore the MeSH database (www.ncbi.nlm.nih .gov/entrez/query.fcgi?db=mesh) for other useful subject headings relevant to a particular interest. Combined with other subject terms of interest and free text search strategies, the above vocabulary should enable a beginning *MEDLINE* user to dig deeply into the literature.

BIOSIS

BIOSIS is a core bibliographic database for biology. It is derived from *Biological Abstracts*, though with additional technical report and conference paper content. Compared to *MEDLINE*, *BIOSIS* offers greater coverage of non-journal literature, including conference paper abstracts, technical reports, and book chapters. *BIOSIS* is of particular importance in plant biology, comparative biology, and evolution/systematics, subject areas that are incompletely covered in *MEDLINE*.

A controlled vocabulary system exists in *BIOSIS*, though it is generally not as powerful as the MeSH vocabulary because of inconsistent application of terms to records in the database and significant redundancies in the vocabulary itself. (The vocabulary includes many author-supplied subject terms and keywords.) One strength of *BIOSIS*, though, is the strong implementation of Linnaean biological classification in the database records. Hence, for searching the literature concerning a particular species of interest (especially species not commonly studied in biomedical laboratories), *BIOSIS* is an excellent starting point.

SciFinder Scholar

SciFinder Scholar is the online interface to the literature database produced by the Chemical Abstracts Service of the American Chemical Society, and it is the bibliographic source most relevant to chemistry literature. Journal, conference, and patent literature, as well as books and dissertations relevant to chemistry, the molecular life sciences, and other physical sciences, are well covered. Much of the functionality of this tool revolves around chemical structure, properties, and reaction searching. For example, the substance identifier function can be used to retrieve some *GenBank* records (included in the Chemical Abstracts Service database in association with article records that cite the sequence record). The textual search function of *SciFinder Scholar* is well developed and is unusual in its implementation of a form of natural language processing for search queries. Users are advised to enter queries as full English language phrases, including prepositions as one would in regular speech (e.g., "applications of mass spectrometry to identification of protein mixtures"). Records in *SciFinder Scholar* consist of article abstracts and additional indexing. However, the details of query processing in *SciFinder Scholar* are proprietary, and analysis of the system and its use of record title, abstracts, and indexing to resolve queries is beyond the scope of this chapter. *SciFinder Scholar* is of particular interest to computational biology researchers working in protein structure determination and in proteomics, the high-throughput analysis of protein samples, and in other fields where "wet lab" analytical instrumentation butts up closely against computerized data systems.

Inspec

Inspec is the premier bibliographic database for physics, electrical and computer engineering, computer science, information technology, and systems control. This combination of disciplines makes it well suited to literature searching, specifically in the tool development arena of computational biology, as well as the related specialties of high-throughput genomics and proteomics. *Inspec* comprehensively covers literature from IEEE and ACM, publishers previously mentioned as becoming increasingly invested in computational biology research and publication.

Inspec includes primarily peer-reviewed journal content and conference proceedings. The database utilizes a well-structured hierarchical controlled vocabulary, much like *MEDLINE*, though not as deep in the areas pertinent to computational biology. Relevant terms include biology computing, statistical analysis, data mining, and protein folding.

Biological Databases

In defining the literature of computational biology, the role of websites providing access to various biological data cannot be overlooked. computational biology has, in the view of many biology researchers, extended the functional definition of "literature" in the biomolecular sciences beyond the traditional research article to include database records that contain the results of biological experimentation and analysis. Depending on the types of data contained in these resources (e.g., text, biological sequence, and/or numerical data), biological databases may be productively searched using textual-based or nontextual (e.g., sequence string, numerical) search methods. These database records are often sparse in format and lack the generous exposition or context setting of a traditional research paper. However, as with more traditional literature, the information contained in these databases describes the results of one or more biological experiments and is referenced on a regular basis by other workers, used to inform further experimentation, and considered to be a "statement of record." Many of the better biological databases offer bibliographies or links to the formal journal literature. In many cases, database entries undergo a kind of peer review process, or curation, as part of their deposition into a database.

The number of biological databases allowing access to various specialty data has burgeoned in recent years; as mentioned previously, the journal *Nucleic Acids Research* offers regular updates on various new or enhanced biological databases. Biological databases of canonical importance to the field include *GenBank*, the related *RefSeq* project, the *Protein Data Bank*, and *Online Mendelian Inheritance in Man*.

GenBank

Containing data from 1982 to 2005, *GenBank* (www.ncbi.nlm.nih .gov/Genbank/) is the National Center for Biotechnology Information genetic sequence database.[13] It serves as a repository and access point for the better part of all publicly available DNA sequences. The database continues to grow at exponential rates, thanks in large part to the steady number of high-throughput genome sequencing projects underway for numerous organisms. Molecular biology researchers have been expected for many years to submit to *GenBank* the novel sequences they determine or produce in the course of their research; specifically, submission of the sequence information on sequences referred to in research reports is frequently a publication requirement for journals in molecular biology. Compatible formatting and daily data exchange between *GenBank*, the *European Molecular Biology Laboratory Data Library*, and the *DNA Data Bank of Japan* ensure that these three databases capture sequence data produced worldwide.

While sequences submitted to *GenBank* undergo screening and basic annotation before they are released into the database, *GenBank* is considered an archival, noncurated database. There is consequently considerable variation in the level of annotation provided for various records in *GenBank*, and records can be altered and updated by their submitters in perpetuity following their inclusion. Also, the same genetic sequences are often found in many records in the database where particular stretches of DNA sequence have been studied by multiple groups over time.

RefSeq

These characteristics have led to some compromise in the usability and re-
liability of *GenBank* as a reference information resource, and this deficit led
to development of the *RefSeq*, or Reference Sequence, project at the National
Center for Biotechnology Information (www.ncbi.nlm.nih.gov/RefSeq/).[14]
RefSeq provides a well-annotated set of DNA, RNA, and protein sequences
for a number of model organisms. *RefSeq* records undergo expert curation to
provide a reliable level of detail (e.g., features of the sequence such as alter-
nate processing sites and cataloging of known sequence variations) in each
record. *RefSeq* records also include a comprehensive list of publications related to the subject gene or protein. The database is non-redundant: Only a
single database record for a given gene and organism is present in the database. These features have made the *RefSeq* dataset useful as a reference information source for gene-level data in several model organisms such as mouse
(*Mus musculus*), zebrafish (*Danio rerio*), and fruit fly (*Drosophila
melanogaster*). The dataset is important as a reference point in the annotation
and further study of other genes and organisms. Data in *GenBank* and *RefSeq*
are readily retrieved using the NCBI website with the tools Entrez (a text
search tool) and BLAST (www.ncbi.nlm.nih.gov/BLAST).

Protein Data Bank

The *Protein Data Bank* is a key database for biological structure data.[15]
This database is the premier repository of three-dimensional structure information on proteins and related biological macromolecules. *Protein Data
Bank* records include the experimentally determined three-dimensional coordinates of the individual atoms in a particular biological structure, annotation on structural motifs found in the structural model, details pertaining
to the experimental methods used to determine the structure, and bibliographic references. As with *GenBank*, many research journals require authors to submit experimentally determined protein structures to the *Protein
Data Bank*, in order to publish findings on these structures.

Online Mendelian Inheritance in Man

Online Mendelian Inheritance in Man (*OMIM*) (www.ncbi.nlm.nih.gov/
entrez/query.fcgi?db=OMIM) is a key computational biology database with
close ties to the area of medical informatics.[16] The database is a catalog of
human genetic disorders and their causative genes. Searchable through the
Entrez text search engine (which also serves *PubMed* and many other NCBI
resources), the database serves as a key information source in medically oriented computational biology applications and is useful to basic biomedical

scientists as well. The entries are essentially short reviews of current knowledge on particular genetic disorders and genes and include well-annotated descriptions of gene function, clinical presentation, and references to the journal literature and to related sequence information in *GenBank* and other databases.

LITERATURE SEARCHES IN COMPUTATIONAL BIOLOGY

Research in computational biology may be considered conceptually to fall into two broad arenas. On one hand, many researchers are primarily concerned with the development of algorithms and computational tools for the storage, management, manipulation, and analysis of biological data. Researchers in this arena are primarily concerned with problems of computer science and engineering, information technology, and mathematics and statistics. Of course, a familiarity with relevant biological principles is key in delivering highly useful tools and in communicating with the intended end users, usually biological scientists. On the other hand, other computational biology researchers are at root biologists, chemists, or physicists, primarily interested in the application of computational biology tools to answer biological (or biophysical or biochemical) questions. Again, appreciation of the workings of computational tools from a mathematical and programming viewpoint is of immense value to the biologist in ensuring that tools are used properly, technically valid conclusions are drawn from the computational manipulations, and improvements in systems can be made.

The focus of one's work in computational biology (developer, user, or both) informs the focus of the literature search and the bibliographic sources of primary interest. However, the actual literature does not divide itself neatly into conceptual categories; many authors in computational biology engage in both tool development and actual biological inquiry, so their writing may cross between these arenas. In a comprehensive search, it should be considered that some items of interest will be found in the literature sources of all the parent disciplines, regardless of one's core disciplinary stripe.

The sections below provide a stepwise strategy for accessing and understanding the computational biology literature. Where appropriate, customizations of the process, depending on a researcher's background and interest, are suggested.

Key Monographs of Interest

For researchers new to the field or with significant experience in one of the parent disciplines but not the other (e.g., biology but not computer science), there has been no shortage of introductory monographs and textbooks in computational biology. Some of these works focus on database development and programming skills, while others focus on the use of existing tools in novel biological research, a distinction that is not always immediately apparent from the title of the work. A few recent titles are of particular note. *Current Protocols in Bioinformatics* is a regularly updated online textbook (also available in print in loose-leaf notebook format).[17] Part of the larger Current Protocols series in the biosciences, it is oriented primarily for biologists and covers in considerable detail the use of many frequently used, publicly available sequence analysis tools and other applications. Secondary attention is given to database development concerns. *Bioinformatics: A Practical Guide to the Analysis of Genes and Proteins*, now in its third edition, is similar in scope, though the two works are unique and complementary.[18] The latter includes some introduction to Computational Biology programming in Perl. *Dictionary of Bioinformatics and Computational Biology* offers a useful and up-to-date grounding in the vocabulary of the fields and can be a useful reference to researchers with either a biology or computer science background.[19] *Bioinformatics, Biocomputing, and Perl: An Introduction to Bioinformatics Computing Skills and Practice* is oriented specifically towards biologists new to computer science who aim to develop programming skills.[20]

Programmers and mathematicians seeking exposure to the biological underpinnings of computational biology might seek out introductory biochemistry or molecular biology texts. Numerous titles are available on the market, and the following is a sample of well-known available textbooks. *Biochemistry* is in its third edition and offers a thorough grounding in the chemistry and functionality of DNA, RNA, and proteins.[21] The text offers considerable depth and provides a solid footing for workers focusing on protein and enzyme function and cellular metabolism, though perhaps more detail than needed by many students looking for only a basic introduction. *Molecular Biology of the Gene* concentrates on the "informational molecules" of the cell (e.g., DNA and RNA) and their role in encoding proteins.[22] It is a thorough introduction to the biology of DNA and the processing of genetic information in the cell, which are the areas of focus of most core computational biology research and development. *Molecular Biology of the Cell* is another alternative resource in the area of molecular biology with similar merits.[23]

Use of the Review Literature

Given a basic understanding of the field, the review literature is generally the most fruitful entry point into the computational biology literature. Reviews are typically written with a detailed introduction of the research topic under discussion, defining terms and explaining key concepts. These articles also often provide an overview of how the particular research problems being described relate to the larger field of study. Finally, review articles provide rich bibliographies of the important journal articles and other key writings of interest that have pushed the research area forward.

Most bibliographic databases provide means to limit a literature search to retrieve only review articles, and researchers exploring a new or unfamiliar topic are well advised to make use of this capability for all these reasons.

Use of the Primary Literature

In order to directly assess prior experiments and discoveries, the researcher will eventually need to explore the primary literature. As mentioned, review articles will direct the reader to key references, which can be supplemented with further searches in article index sources. A comprehensive literature search in computational biology should include, at a minimum, search efforts in each of the bibliographic databases described above: *MEDLINE, BIOSIS, SciFinder Scholar*, and *Inspec*. *Inspec* will likely be of most critical use to software and database developers, but its inclusion of physics literature makes it useful in explorations of several areas of biological interest, such as protein folding prediction and biological signal transduction. The bibliographic databases *MEDLINE, BIOSIS*, and *SciFinder Scholar* are of interest both to tool-design specialists and especially to biologically oriented researchers.

To learn the details of particular discoveries or developments, and to effectively search the historical literature, it will often be necessary to revisit indexes multiple times, searching on newly discovered vocabulary terms found while reading review or primary literature. To find the formal documentation of an original discovery, it will also sometimes be necessary to backtrack from an initial reference given in a recent article through the references of several consecutive research papers published over the course of several years.

Exploring Biological Databases

Computational biology researchers interested in biological problems are additionally advised to probe the biological databases (e.g. *RefSeq, Protein Data Bank*, and *OMIM*) as part of their search strategies for further details of the molecules, diseases, and other topics of interest. As alluded, many biological databases contain substantial bibliographies as part of their records, allowing them to be used as an additional entry point into the formal literature.

NOTES

1. F. S. Collins, M. Morgan, and A. Patrinos, "The Human Genome Project: Lessons from Large-Scale Biology," *Science* 300, no. 5617 (April 2003): 286–90.

2. Monica J. Justice, "From the Atomic Age to the Genome Project," *Genetica* 122, no. 1 (September 2004): 3–7.

3. David Fenstermacher, "Introduction to Bioinformatics," *Journal of the American Society for Information Science and Technology* 56, no. 5 (March 2005): 440–46.

4. *MeSH Database*, "Computational Biology," 1999, at www.ncbi.nlm.nih.gov/entrez/query.fcgi?db=mesh (accessed August 30, 2005).

5. *Oxford Reference Online: A Dictionary of Biology*, "Bioinformatics," 2006, at www.oxfordreference.com/views/ENTRY.html?subview=Main&entry=t6.e5813 (accessed April 10, 2005).

6. Hagit Shatkay and Ronen Feldman, "Mining the Biomedical Literature in the Genomic Era: An Overview," *Journal of Computational Biology* 10, no. 6 (December 2003): 821–55.

7. S. B. Needleman and C. D. Wunsch, "A General Method Applicable to the Search for Similarities in the Amino Acid Sequence of Two Proteins," *Journal of Molecular Biology* 48, no. 3 (March 1970): 443–53.

8. Temple F. Smith and Michael S. Waterman, "Identification of Common Molecular Subsequences," *Journal of Molecular Biology* 147, no. 1 (March 1981): 195–97.

9. Barbara A. Rapp and David L. Wheeler, "Bioinformatics Resources from the National Center for Biotechnology Information: An Integrated Foundation for Discovery," *Journal of the American Society for Information Science and Technology* 56, no. 5 (March 2005): 538–50.

10. S. E. Altschul and others, "Basic Local Alignment Search Tool," *Journal of Molecular Biology* 215, no. 3 (October 1990): 403–10.

11. Christy Hightower, "Science and Technology Sources on the Internet," *Issues in Science and Technology Librarianship* 33 (Winter 2002).

12. National Library of Medicine Fact Sheet, "What's the Difference between MEDLINE and PubMed?" December 21, 2004, at www.nlm.nih.gov/pubs/factsheets/dif_med_pub.html (accessed August 30, 2005).

13. Dennis A. Benson and others, "GenBank: Update," *Nucleic Acids Research* 32, no. 1 (January 2004): D23–26.

14. Kim D. Pruitt, Tatiana Tatusova, and Donna R. Maglott, "NCBI Reference Sequence (RefSeq): A Curated Non-redundant Sequence Database of Genomes, Transcripts and Proteins," *Nucleic Acids Research* 33, no. 1 (January 2005): D501–4.

15. Nita Deshpande and others, "The RCSB Protein Data Bank: A Redesigned Query System and Relational Database Based on the mmCIF Schema," *Nucleic Acids Research* 33, no. 1 (January 2005): D233–37.

16. Ada Hamosh and others, "Online Mendelian Inheritance in Man (OMIM): A Knowledgebase of Human Genes and Genetic Disorders," *Nucleic Acids Research* 33, no. 1 (January 2005): D514–17.

17. Andreas D. Baxevanis, *Current Protocols in Bioinformatics* (New York: Wiley, 2003).

18. Andreas D. Baxevanis and B. F. Francis Ouellette, *Bioinformatics: A Practical Guide to the Analysis of Genes and Proteins*, 3rd ed. (Hoboken, NJ: Wiley, 2005).

19. John M. Hancock and Marketa J. Zvelebil, *Dictionary of Bioinformatics and Computational Biology* (Hoboken, NJ: Wiley-Liss, 2004).

20. Michael Moorhouse and Paul Barry, *Bioinformatics, Biocomputing, and Perl: An Introduction to Bioinformatics Computing Skills and Practice* (Hoboken, NJ: Wiley, 2004).

21. Donald Voet and Judith Voet, *Biochemistry*, 3rd ed. (Hoboken, NJ: Wiley, 2004).

22. James D. Watson, *Molecular Biology of the Gene*, 5th ed. (San Francisco: Pearson/Benjamin Cummings, 2004).

23. Bruce Alberts, *Molecular Biology of the Cell*, 4th ed. (New York: Garland, 2002).

9

Engineering Entrepreneurship

Yoo-Seong Song

The term "engineering entrepreneurship" is used interchangeably with "technology entrepreneurship" by scholars and practitioners. Shaker A. Zahra and James C. Hayton define technology entrepreneurship as "the creation of new firms by independent entrepreneurs and corporations to exploit technological discoveries."[1] While entrepreneurship is an umbrella term that includes both technology-based and non-technology-based firms, engineering entrepreneurship specifically refers to entrepreneurial activities that are strictly based on new technologies or scientific findings. Non-technology-based firms are founded based on new business concepts that utilize existing technologies. For example, those that establish new companies to provide financial services via the Internet are considered non-technology-based entrepreneurs, since the core of their business is financial services, not technology. On the other hand, those that provide innovative financial transaction systems to be used for various financial services firms doing business via the Internet can be categorized as technology-based entrepreneurs. The rapid growth of engineering entrepreneurship programs and centers at universities demonstrates the new wave of commercializing technology discoveries, which increasingly have significant economic and social implications.

HISTORY AND DEVELOPMENT OF ENTREPRENEURSHIP

Economist Joseph A. Schumpeter, perhaps the most influential figure in entrepreneurship research, introduced an idea of "creative destruction" that described an entrepreneur disrupting an existing market by injecting innovations or technological breakthroughs.[2] As a result, new products, manufacturing processes, or even new markets and industries would be born. Schumpeter viewed entrepreneurs as providing the source of economic growth by continuously bringing innovations to the market that would otherwise remain stagnant.

Since World War II, the field of entrepreneurship has increasingly received attention from scholars. Its growth is evident in the increasing number of publications and proliferation of entrepreneurship programs at academic institutions, especially after the mid-1980s. Diverse disciplines, ranging from economics and management, to psychology and sociology, to engineering, and to public policy have examined entrepreneurship in their own perspectives. As a result, entrepreneurship is generally regarded as interdisciplinary in nature. The number of journals specifically devoted to entrepreneurship has increased significantly in the past two decades, reflecting the rapid maturity of this field.

Although much of the early research focused on personal traits of entrepreneurs, research topics have gradually diversified. Early research sought to understand the entrepreneurs as individuals with regards to their behavior in starting and running their own businesses. The focus on entrepreneurs as individuals has shifted to different aspects of entrepreneurship, such as the process of establishing new firms, the role of the government in promoting innovations through small businesses, the importance of geographic proximities among new firms for knowledge and resource sharing, the knowledge transfer between universities and companies, and the financing of new ventures. However, researchers from diverse disciplines often study entrepreneurship without strong collaborations, and for this reason, Donald L. Sexton and Hans Landstrom call this field "un-disciplinary," rather than interdisciplinary.[3] The proliferation of research done on entrepreneurship in a variety of disciplines necessitates developing a common theoretical framework to foster collaboration among researchers.

Universities have rapidly adopted entrepreneurship in their business programs either as course offerings or degree concentrations. In 1947, Harvard University offered the first M.B.A. entrepreneurship courses in the United States, later followed by New York University and Stanford University. The adoption of entrepreneurship in the higher education curriculums has accelerated since the 1970s. The nation's first entrepreneurship center was established by Southern Methodist University in 1970, while the University of Southern California offered the nation's first M.B.A. and undergraduate concentration in entrepreneurship in 1972 and 1976, respectively. Furthermore, academic conferences and associations focusing on entrepreneurship began to form during the 1970s. However, although universities across the nation are now offering entrepreneurship course offerings or concentrations at the bachelor's and master's levels, the number of doctoral programs in entrepreneurship remains relatively small.[4]

A growing number of universities are offering entrepreneurship centers and programs that are primarily based in engineering schools, which speaks to the facts that innovation is the key factor of entrepreneurship, and innovation is driven by the latest engineering and science discoveries. This deviates from a traditional model in which entrepreneurship centers at universities are housed in and run by business schools. The main goal of engineering entrepreneurship is to help engineers and scientists become entrepreneurs, whereas the primary audience of traditional entrepreneurship programs is business students.

In general, engineers and scientists are not trained well in business concepts. Martin observed a traditional "management aversion" by engineers and scientists, and it resulted in limited, if any, collaboration between business and engineering schools. Engineering entrepreneurship amends such a break between management and technology, since successful technology entrepreneurs need to be competent not only in technology, but also in business management skills.

In addition to course offerings and degree programs in engineering entrepreneurship, universities are also active in commercializing new technologies developed by their faculty and students. Universities often work with state governments or individual investors to provide seed money to fund engineering faculty to launch new companies. It is well-known that Stanford University played a central role in the evolution of Silicon Valley. Engineering entrepreneurship in the form of a university-industry alliance is a mutually beneficial relationship. Universities provide the expertise of engineering faculty and students, and companies offer industry knowledge. Universities can secure funding for their research activities, while companies can obtain access to new technologies without incurring high personnel costs.[5]

In addition to universities, many local governments have acknowledged the significance and impact of engineering entrepreneurship on their local economies. Successful technology-based companies attract financial capital to the state and create new jobs; thus state governments actively seek ways to help such emerging technology companies.

LITERATURE SEARCH STRATEGIES
FOR ENGINEERING ENTREPRENEURSHIP

Patents

As a need for a product is perceived, the first step is to determine if the product or similar products have already been patented to avoid patent infringement. Searching patent information is very complex; many inventors hire patent attorneys to do a thorough search. Without being patented, new technologies will be extremely difficult to commercialize and can easily be copied and used by other companies without any legal and financial obligations.

The United States Patent and Trademark Office (USPTO) examines patent applications for granting patent rights. It also maintains a public database of patents that have been issued, as well as applications currently in review. The USPTO's database (www.uspto.gov) offers detailed descriptions, names of the inventors, diagrams, and specifications of the inventions.

Patents issued since 1976 can be searched by using an inventor's name, keywords, an application date, or patent number, while only a classification or patent number can be used to search for patents issued between 1790 and 1975. Patents issued from 1872 to 2002 can also be located by searching the printed *Official Gazette of the United States Patent Office.*

Primary Research Literature

The second step is to search for primary literature such as journal articles, conference papers, and books. Searching the engineering literature provides insights into current research that may relate to the new technology being investigated. When new technologies are developed, inventors usually apply for patents first and then publish their findings. Literature searches also help researchers discover potential applications of similar technologies as performed and suggested by other researchers. Research literature is the best way to keep current on the latest technological developments. For example, the Institute of Electrical and Electronics Engineers (IEEE) produces the latest research in computer and electrical engineering, and its conference proceedings deal with a variety of issues, including engineering entrepreneurship. IEEE maintains an electronic database of past and current proceedings.

Compendex is the major electronic index for engineering. It is equivalent to the printed *Engineering Index,* which covers the literature back to 1884. *Compendex* covers over 5,000 engineering-related information publications, such as scholarly journals, conference proceedings, and trade journals. By using index databases such as *Compendex,* researchers can easily locate and retrieve citations to these publications (including IEEE).

ABI/INFORM is the major electronic index to the business literature. It covers the most comprehensive list of business journals and newspapers. *ABI/INFORM* offers access to citations and full texts of articles that provide the latest information on business techniques, industry environment, companies, international trades, and consumer behaviors. It is especially known for its abstracting and indexing a huge amount of articles, so researchers can easily identify and locate relevant materials. The database offers access to industry journals, scholarly journals, and also regional news publications. *ABI/INFORM* is available in various formats, including Internet subscription or CD-ROM.

Although there is no scholarly journal that is exclusively devoted to engineering entrepreneurship yet, most journals on general entrepreneurship contain a significant number of articles dealing with technology issues. In 1949, Harvard published the first journal devoted to entrepreneurship, *Explorations in Entrepreneurial History*, but it ceased publication in 1969. In 1963, the *Journal of Small Business Management* was started by the National Council for Small Business Management Development (now called the International Council for Small Business), and it is still one of the most highly regarded journals, covering such topics as franchising, management of small and family businesses, legal implications for small businesses, and venture creation. Since then, an increasing number of journals began publishing in the area of entrepreneurship, especially during the 1990s. As of 2001, Jerome A. Katz reported that forty-four refereed journals devoted to entrepreneurship research are in publication. According to him, there are five core scholarly journals in the area of entrepreneurship covered: *Social Sciences Citation Index*: *Journal of Business Venturing, Journal of Small Business Management, Small Business Economics, Entrepreneurship and Regional Development*, and *Entrepreneurship: Theory and Practice*.[6]

The growth of popular and trade journals in entrepreneurship has been faster than that of scholarly journals. Popular and trade journals provide the latest trends and news in the field of entrepreneurship and technology management. *Entrepreneur* magazine started in 1976 followed by *Inc.* magazine in 1979. Considered to be the premier magazines for entrepreneurship, both publications offer current insight in the latest technologies, management, marketing, and finance issues. Similarly, newsletters from national and regional venture capital associations provide the latest developments in engineering and technology discoveries, venture capital trends, and entrepreneurship. There are numerous popular and trade journals devoted to specific types of technology, such as IT, software, semiconductor, robotics, and medical technologies.

Market Research

The third step in the research strategy is to gather market research. Market research helps the entrepreneur learn the current state of the market with the existing technology by determining the competition, supplier relationship, consumer behavior or preference, and government regulations. Once the uniqueness and market potential of the new technology has been investigated, the entrepreneur will need to possess in-depth understanding of the market environment to attract financial capital and fund further growth of the firm or business venture. Engineering entrepreneurship is a combination of technological breakthroughs and business skills, and a thorough analysis of the market is necessary to develop business plans. A business plan is a document that illustrates the company's objectives, current financial state and future forecast, needed resources to achieve the objectives, and short- and long-term strategies.

One difficulty that entrepreneurs often encounter is the lack of information to assess the market potential of new technologies. In many cases, entrepreneurs develop technologies where no market yet exists, and markets that do not exist cannot be analyzed with insufficient information. Thus, entrepreneurs need to collect information on related markets and technologies. In doing so, they can learn about current structures and the environment of the existing markets and assess opportunities and risks for their innovations. Based on the results from market research, entrepreneurs can determine potential customers, product component manufacturers, distributors, and marketing strategies.

Resources for market research are abundant for various types of industries. Industry-specific information resources—such as industry journals and newspapers and professional associations—are excellent sources of information, as they provide industry-specific statistics and outlook analysis. Using the *ABI/INFORM* database, researchers can retrieve citations to articles on various markets from a wide variety of information resources and determine market factors, such as potential competitors, customers, challenges, and opportunities. *Thomas Register* has established its reputation by providing information on industrial products, brands, and manufacturers, and it now covers over 165,000 manufacturers from the United States and Canada. This database can be used to develop a list of component manufacturers or even a list of potential competitors.

Standards, Guidelines, and Regulations

The fourth step is to search for applicable standards. When engineers design new products or processes, they need to follow common guidelines to ensure that the products, processes, and services meet the minimum level of quality. Standards help increase productivity and interoperability. Standards and regulations are developed by professional societies, government agencies, and other national and international organizations.

Among the most frequently used standards are those issued by the International Organization for Standardization, the American National Standards Institute (ANSI), the American Society for Testing and Materials (ASTM), the National Institute of Standards and Technology (NIST), and the IEEE. The National Standards Systems Network offers a database of references to standards developed by organizations like ANSI, private sector standard organizations, government agencies, and international organizations available for sale. The ASTM and NIST also offer online search capabilities of their standards databases via their Internet websites.

CONCLUSION

Engineering entrepreneurship is a rapidly growing field. Universities now offer courses and degree programs in engineering entrepreneurship. In addition, they establish support centers to manage new technological innovations and accelerate commercialization of promising new technologies. Governments also show a strong interest in this field, since new technology startup companies can potentially stimulate the local economy by creating jobs and bringing in revenues. Literature searching on engineering entrepreneurship is complex, because the literature on this topic is widely scattered. When conducting a literature search, one has to carefully establish the scope of research to identify appropriate information sources.

NOTES

1. Shaker A. Zahra and James C. Hayton, "Technological Entrepreneurship: Key Themes and Emerging Research Directions," in *Crossroads of Entrepreneurship*, ed. Guido Corbetta, Morten Huse, and Davide Ravasi (Boston: Kluwer Academic Publishers, 2004), 185.

2. Joseph A. Schumpeter, *Capitalism, Socialism, and Democracy*, (New York: Harper and Brothers, 1942), 83.

3. Donald L. Sexton and Hans Landstrom, eds., *The Blackwell Handbook of Entrepreneurship* (Oxford, UK: Blackwell Scientific Publications, 2000), xxi.

4. Jerome A. Katz, "The Chronology and Intellectual Trajectory of American Entrepreneurship Education," *Journal of Business Venturing* 18, no. 2 (March 2003): 286–90.

5. Zahra and Hayton, "Technological Entrepreneurship: Key Themes and Emerging Research Directions," 199–200.

6. Jerome A. Katz, "Core Publications in Entrepreneurship and Related Fields: A Guide to Getting Published," *Entrepreneurship Education on the Web*, June 24, 2003, at eweb.slu.edu/booklist.htm (accessed February 23, 2005).

10

Machine Learning

Tracy Gabridge

Machine learning is a field deeply rooted in the realm of computer science, which also encompasses artificial intelligence, robotics, natural language processing, and others. Its research culture follows these fields very closely, though it has had interdisciplinary influences since its very beginning. An examination of machine learning as an interdisciplinary field can serve as an interesting case study for fields that lie within the superstructure of computer science. Aspects brought out here about where machine learning intersects with other disciplines can illuminate similar aspects about the other related fields. This chapter will examine how machine learning evolved as a distinct field and how its interdisciplinary influences have changed over time. This chapter also includes a discussion of components of the literature, along with a description of how to best discover literature in machine learning and its related fields.

THE EVOLUTION OF MACHINE LEARNING RESEARCH

Interdisciplinary research in machine learning has proven to be an evolving science, where the areas of overlap with other research fields have changed over time from one area to another as the field matures and grows. Even as the field of machine learning is firmly rooted in the larger realm of Computer Science, major influences from psychology, business, and mathematics create a field that is multifaceted and rich for examination by new researchers.

To understand how to efficiently and thoroughly conduct a literature search in machine learning, it is helpful to start at the origins of the field.

The field of machine learning concerns itself with creating systems that can demonstrate improvement over time in performance, thus showing that the machine has learned without being programmed explicitly to improve on the task. Human learning methods from the field of cognitive science within the discipline of psychology provide many models that have fueled the machine learning field from the very beginning, whether learning by example, induction, case-based methods, clustering, and so on. But despite the fact that artificial intelligence and cognitive science got their start in the middle part of the twentieth century, it took several decades for machine learning to emerge as an individual and distinct field from its parents.

It is widely accepted that artificial intelligence and cognitive science became distinct fields in the 1950s. In 1950, A. M. Turing wrote the article "Computing Machinery and Intelligence," in which he discusses the education and learning of a child program.[1] The capability of machines to learn has been a key concept in artificial intelligence from its beginning. Cognitive science, on the other hand, was concerned with understanding the human aspects of cognition, including learning. A tenet held in common in the two fields was that "Learning was viewed as a central feature of intelligent systems."[2] In artificial intelligence, researchers envisioned an intelligent computer system, while the cognitive scientists endeavored to understand nothing less than the operating system of humankind.

The 1950s and 1960s marked a time of exploration into computational models of human intelligence. Rather than concentrate on computational learning, artificial intelligence researchers worked "to understand the role of knowledge in human behavior."[3] Artificial intelligence work was largely inspired by "neurophysiological, biological and psychological research."[4] Early models of brain functioning were created using nonlinear, networked elements that spawned the research area of neural networks. Computational techniques later generated in this area were highly useful to machine learning researchers.[5]

After the theoretical underpinnings forged in the 1960s, the 1970s brought focused work and development of practical algorithms with a machine learning flavor within computer science. While still hoping to model human learning, the field grew past "domain-specific emphasis of expert systems" and experienced excitement about "the prospect of automating the acquisition of domain-specific knowledge-bases."[6] This era also saw demonstrations of machine learning on interesting tasks in areas as diverse as spectrometry, the diagnosis of soybean diseases, and chess playing.[7]

The 1980s marked the emergence of machine learning as a distinct field. By this time, much work had been done expanding on the theories of the 1960s and the practical algorithms of the 1970s and allowed knowledge representation and performance to coalesce into a research agenda focused on learning. In the 1980s, there was a retrenchment to focus on enhancing specific areas within computer science.[8] Machine learning was one of these areas. By 1980, there was such a critical mass of machine learning researchers that thirty of them held their first conference at Carnegie Mellon University.[9]

The 1980s also witnessed an expansion in research directions in machine learning. Practical uses of machine learning algorithms became apparent, as computing power began to be more widely available. Now applied machine learning methods became prominent alongside the theoretical research efforts. With this expansion, the interdisciplinary connections also grew. Beyond cognitive science, operations research fields became interested in data mining, knowledge discovery and databases, and case-based expert systems. Research in adaptive control theory in the 1980s also influenced research in machine learning. Nils J. Nilsson says, "Control theorists study the problem of controlling a process having unknown parameters which must be estimated during operation."[10] The problems they study are directly related to the problems—investigated by machine learning researchers—where inputs and other factors can change in a learning environment.

Since then, the field has continued to grow in both theoretical and practical realms. The first conference that originally attracted thirty attendees now boasts more than three hundred, and the number of places where machine learning researchers can present their work has grown as well. As the field has developed, the interdisciplinary connections have also continued to change. Reference citations in research papers show a shift from the inclusion of papers on cognitive science to those from statistics. In the 1990s and the early years of the twenty-first century, the field of statistics emerged as a distinct contributing factor in current machine learning research.[11] Today, the machine learning field is beginning to see an influx of scientists from statistics contributing to current research.

While there are many intersecting interdisciplinary influences in the field of machine learning, it is interesting to note that machine learning has proceeded separately but largely in parallel with cognitive science. As cognitive science has evolved over the years, computational neuroscience and neural information processing fields have emerged as distinct entities. Today, researchers from both machine learning and computational neuroscience meet and present at some of the same conferences because they share similar statistical methods, even though their research interests may not overlap in significant ways anymore. While a few researchers from each field publish in the others' domain, most publish within their fields' established publications.

MACHINE LEARNING AS A DISTINCT RESEARCH AREA

The fields of machine learning and artificial intelligence both lean "towards symbolic representations rather than numeric ones," and they both use "heuristic approaches to learning rather than algorithmic ones."[12] Both are problem driven rather than technique driven. While artificial intelligence concerns itself with intelligence in the broadest sense, machine learning finds its niche in a more narrow area, in systems that learn over time to improve their performance.

As machine learning was evolving, its research was distinct from cognitive science simply in terms of the system that is doing the learning—machine versus human. Today, the style in which the research is done is different. Cognitive science approaches an "attempt to develop empirically-based theories of learning, while research in machine learning takes a more formal-constructive tack in developing theories and models of learning phenomena."[13] Also, the end result of machine learning research is not intended to illuminate the way humans learn, but rather to make better machines and programs. Thus, machine learning researchers do not have a research imperative that compels them to expose their findings to the cognitive science researchers. On the other hand, the cognitive science researchers might find that the machine learning community has found some interesting cognitive models that may shed light on replicating human methods of learning. However, since methods and results are different, the two fields have not melded as much as expected.

Several professional societies support research in the machine learning field. Since machine learning is closely related to artificial intelligence, the American Association for Artificial Intelligence (AAAI) supports the field under its broad umbrella. Founded in 1979, AAAI supports the field by providing conferences, workshops, and a significant publishing outlet for researchers. Their goals are to advance "the scientific understanding of the mechanisms underlying thought and intelligent behavior" and "to increase public understanding of Artificial Intelligence, improve the teaching and training of Artificial Intelligence practitioners, and provide guidance for research planners and funders concerning the importance and potential of current Artificial Intelligence developments."[14] AAAI conferences are quite large, and machine learning fills one track within the overall society structure. At one recent conference, more than 450 papers were submitted for review; there were about 190 papers and demonstrations, and approximately two dozen related explicitly to machine learning. European and Pacific Rim societies exist to fulfill a similar purpose for their regional artificial intelligence researchers. Overarching all of these is the International Joint Conferences on Artificial Intelligence, which gathers together researchers around the world at its biennial conferences. The focus of the conference is broad, so machine learning occupies a few tracks among many at this very large meeting.

In the years since machine learning became an identifiable field, other societies have appeared and serve the needs of this specific community. The International Machine Learning Society came into existence in the past few years to sponsor the International Conference of Machine Learning. This conference is traditionally run concurrently with the Association for Computing Machinery Conference on Computational Learning Theory and Uncertainty in AI.

STRUCTURE OF MACHINE LEARNING LITERATURE

The mission of professional societies involved in areas related to machine learning is to foster interaction among researchers through conferences, symposia, and workshops. Because of this, conferences are vitally important in the machine learning field, and proceedings are valuable sources of information.

Also highly valued are articles published in well-regarded journals. Before the 1980s, machine learning researchers published primarily in artificial intelligence journals. However, as the machine learning community grew, it found that an insufficient number of articles on machine learning topics appeared in the general artificial intelligence journals, even though the number of research topics within the field of machine learning was expanding at a terrific rate. For these reasons, the first journal published solely on machine learning, aptly called *machine learning*, began publication in 1986. Today there are several journals that serve the machine learning community, most notably *Journal of Machine Learning Research*; *Machine Learning*; *IEEE Transactions on Pattern Analysis and Machine Intelligence*; *IEEE Transactions on Systems, Man and Cybernetics*; *Data Mining and Knowledge Discovery*; and *Journal of Artificial Intelligence Research*.

Understanding how to locate the article literature from both conferences and journals in machine learning is crucial, because these two types of publications comprise the vast majority of the literature in the field. The field is evolving so rapidly that journal articles on machine learning can be considered outdated within five years or so. The life span of journal articles within artificial intelligence is generally under ten years. In comparison, journal articles in the field of statistics and probability are still useful after ten years.[15]

Another reason the publication sources discussed thus far cover the field so well is that machine learning researchers are open to input from other fields. However, they traditionally publish quite narrowly within the literature that caters to machine learning and rarely pursue publishing opportunities outside of that area. Until recently, the field primarily attracted people interested in artificial intelligence rather than scholars from other disciplines. Also, as noted previously, machine learning researchers are interested in making machines and software work more effectively and do not find it necessary to expose their work to other areas in order to further their research agendas.[16]

Other information sources important in Machine Learning are dissertations, technical reports, and books. Recent dissertations can be an effective means of understanding the state of the art in the machine learning arena. Generally, one can expect dissertations to be of high quality reviewed quite thoroughly. Technical reports satisfy a variety of needs to disseminate research findings. Some are written to satisfy the terms and conditions of receiving research funding. Some might be written to get the word out quickly about a line of research. A technical report might also provide a place to publish a more extensive set of data or code than can reasonably fit in a journal or conference paper. Some may be written because a paper has not been accepted for publication elsewhere. Generally the technical report literature is more difficult to locate, and more evaluative work might be needed to ensure the quality of the report before using it. Books on machine learning tend to summarize research and compile related results into a single volume. For historical treatments and overviews of specific areas of machine learning, books are an excellent place to start.

One aspect that characterizes papers published on machine learning from those currently published on other, related fields is that machine learning papers are uniformly available in electronic form and can be found on the Internet. A machine learning researcher can typically find a paper of interest within the field at the Internet website of the author or institution (regardless of how the paper was originally published). Given that machine learning researchers are typically interested in material published within the past five years, it is also highly likely that their favorite journal or conference proceedings are also published in electronic form. This characteristic is common throughout computer science research, but is much less common in other fields. For researchers in machine learning trying to find the literature from a related field, like statistics, adaptive control, or cognitive science, traditional means are sometimes necessary for finding the text of an article. Traditional means can encompass using typical library indexes for locating journal articles or conference proceedings that are only available in a print format. This is especially true for older materials.

THOROUGH LITERATURE
SEARCHING IN MACHINE LEARNING

Current information research practices in the field of machine learning follow certain patterns and modes of inquiry that are common across many of the fields of computer science. This section includes a discussion of current practice for finding literature in machine learning and in the parts of the field that touch other disciplines.

A new researcher may be introduced to the field and its literature by reading classic textbooks, which outline major theories and basic research in the field. Two good introductory books in machine learning are *Elements of Machine Learning*[17] and *Readings in Machine Learning*.[18]

Clearly the challenge is to exploit the literature that exists in machine learning and its related disciplines in a way that builds perspective in the field; balances efficiency, speed, and innovation; and maximizes the time a researcher has to spend on the problem at hand. The following are other avenues that can be taken to broaden a new machine learning researcher's information scope.

One issue related to interdisciplinary literature research is that different fields have differing literature practices. Fields like machine learning exist at one extreme of the literature spectrum. Researchers expect that the field is moving so rapidly that older literature may not be as valuable in today's research environment. The literature of mathematics, on the other hand, which encompasses the statistics field, has very different characteristics. Mathematical knowledge builds quite deliberately on its preceding research, and the literature published many years ago can still be relevant today. As one would expect, these extremes necessitate different strategies to effectively mine the literature for relevant pieces of information. Between these two extremes exist the other fields with which machine learning intersects. Adaptive control, cognitive science, and operations research fall within these two end points of the information literature spectrum. Another central literature resource for computer science and, hence, machine learning is conference proceedings. Conference proceedings are an important part of machine learning literature, while in its related fields, journal articles are the primary means of scientific communication.

For researchers unfamiliar with the field, subject searching is the best strategy to use at the beginning of a search. In most cases, one or more authors specializing in a topic will be found. The citation database *Web of Science* offers an alternative method of searching for articles. Using an author's name, one can explore the literature by tracing citations forward and backward, revealing the citations an author used in his own work and discovering who cited that author's work. This index does not meet the needs of machine learning researchers in particular, because it covers only the journal literature. The entire realm of conference literature is not included.

The discipline of computer science has another option, *CiteSeer*, which is a "scientific literature digital library that aims to improve the dissemination and feedback of scientific literature, and to provide improvements in functionality, usability, availability, cost, comprehensiveness, efficiency and timeliness."[19] This index can automatically harvest papers found on the

Internet or can accept submissions from authors. Once a paper is in the database, its cited references are automatically linked. The database contains more than 700,000 papers in the realm of computer science. However, *CiteSeer* does not serve a broad range of subjects, and a paper outside of computer science will only occasionally appear. In addition, *CiteSeer* has some limitations because of the way it searches the database. When performing a keyword search, it is easy to retrieve a large number of articles but difficult to retrieve a precise set of results.

Relying solely on computer science indexes to find machine learning research poses a significant risk of missing highly relevant prior research. Many other indexes exist that cover machine learning and its related fields. The *Inspec* database, created by the Institution of Electrical Engineers, is a significant source for finding journal articles and conference papers in engineering, physics, computer science, communications, and control. For topics related to cognitive science, *PsycINFO* covers the peer-reviewed journals in that field. *MathSciNet* is a likely source to find statistical approaches that may be useful to machine learning. Databases like *Business Source Elite* and the premier engineering source, *Compendex,* can bring out different aspects of knowledge discovery and data mining within machine learning than traditional computer science sources.

Finding other types of literature such as dissertations, technical reports, or books requires other indexes for searching, since the databases highlighted thus far tend to include primarily article literature. One of the main ways to find theses from other institutions is through a database called *Dissertation Abstracts*. *Dissertation Abstracts* includes theses from most fields of research, including machine learning and all of its complementary fields.

Technical reports are useful in the information-gathering phase of any research project. Funding sources often require progress updates and other reports to document the ongoing research that is accomplished with the funding. These reports can give a different and perhaps more comprehensive account than might be found in a corresponding journal article on the same topic. Sometimes technical reports are covered in the standard index databases already mentioned, such as *Inspec,* but usually those resources are not the best finding tools for this type of literature. The *National Technical Information Service* database is one of the major forums for searching for technical report literature that is written in response to government funding sources. Finding technical reports written in response to other funding sources or filling other needs may be somewhat more difficult. Technical reports written for that purpose are not necessarily included in the traditional tools already discussed. Sometimes technical reports written within a company or corporation might be considered proprietary information and may be impossible to get outside of the company. Some elusive technical reports might be found, however, using some of the same methods one might use to find books.

Sometimes books are overlooked as valuable contributors to the information environment that includes multiples disciplines. Occasionally, the main interdisciplinary influence in a particular line of research in machine learning may be a certain statistical technique or certain adaptive control mechanisms. In these cases, it is possible to satisfy that need with a book covering the basics of a field. Finding books is a straightforward process. Most research institutions support sophisticated library systems that purchase materials for research programs. Library catalogs contain the inventory of those systems and can be searched in a multitude of ways. Library catalogs, like several of the tools mentioned thus far, are broad in their holdings, so a specialized field like machine learning will be covered as well as its related disciplines. If a particular institution does not have a certain book, most library systems can obtain the book from another library, usually through a service called inter-library borrowing or something similar. There are also super catalogs that compile the contents of many libraries' catalogs into a single searchable interface that can help in the search for books, technical reports, and dissertations. One prime example in North America is the *WorldCat* database. It contains catalog records from thousands of institutions for a grand total of more than 40 million records. Again, the coverage for this type of tool is incredibly broad and can serve a specialized need within machine learning, but also helps to find information in its related fields.

The searching tools discussed thus far cover their topical areas for a finite range of years in an online format. Most databases that cover machine learning specifically contain resources that span the entire lifetime of the field or will soon do so. For instance, the database *Inspec* currently covers electrical engineering and computer science literature back to the late nineteenth century. While the "classic" literature of machine learning can usually be found through citation searching, the essential documents from machine learning's related fields may not be discovered quite as reliably. One facet of machine learning research that may fall into this territory is statistical research. Since the articles in mathematics journals can remain useful for so long, in order to find important documents published before the time period covered by *MathSciNet* (1940–2005), one of the important mathematics databases, it may be necessary to consult the print versions of the databases.

Knowing the right tools for the job of searching is half the battle for finding high-quality information. The other half is knowing how to use the tools. Fortunately, several simple principles can be applied across the majority of the tools already discussed. The first principle is to take advantage of the standardized terms that are used within a tool to group information resources according to subject area using common language. Once an article, book, or other resource is found that looks promising, a searcher can use the subject terms assigned to that item to find others like it.

One of the most common problems with searching any of the online indexes that exist today is retrieving too many records from a keyword search. It is not too hard to construct an effective search within a field with which a researcher is familiar. However, when branching outside of one's familiar subjects, it may not be as easy to exploit the different vocabulary that exists in that field to discover a highly precise list of relevant documents. The first task is to determine the ways in which a concept is expressed in the field. Finding a topical handbook or well-written textbook in a field can help one become familiar with the terms and structure of research within that field. A good resource for learning the fundamentals of control theory is *Introduction to Control Theory, Including Optimal Control* by Burghes and Graham.[20] Another method is to conduct keyword explorations in any one of the specialized indexes already discussed. Examine the records you find to see other subject terms assigned to that record that might extend your reach into the literature of the field.

While reading handbooks and excellent textbooks is a great method for getting up to speed in a new discipline, examining general review or survey articles found within article databases is also essential for rapid learning on a topic. For an example within machine learning, see the 1996 article "Reinforcement Learning: A Survey" by Kaelbling, Littman, and Moore.[21] This type of article summarizes key issues in the new field and places them in a context that is difficult to get from articles found through topical keyword searches. Review articles can be excellent springboards from which to dive into a new area of research. From a review article, one can often examine the references to get a sense of who the influential thinkers are in that research area. This opens up the possibility of doing author or citation searching on any interesting findings to delve more deeply into a topic.

CONCLUSION

In a recent issue of *Mechanical Engineering* an author noted, "The most surprising discoveries have been made at the boundaries of different disciplines."[22] Many parts of machine learning have advanced at the intersections of artificial intelligence, statistics, cognitive science, and others. Advances in reinforcement learning could not happen without knowledge and use of statistical techniques. Neural networks research would not exist without its beginnings in brain modeling. Machine learning as an interdisciplinary field is quite intriguing, with its high value placed on innovation and its reliance on a broad network of interrelated research areas. The tools and techniques outlined in this chapter will help any new machine learning researcher explore and efficiently take advantage of the many resources available that can illuminate and extend the boundaries of the field.

NOTES

1. A. M. Turing, "Computing Machinery and Intelligence," *Mind* 59, no. 236 (October 1950): 433–60.

2. Pat Langley, *Elements of Machine Learning* (San Francisco: Morgan Kaufmann, 1996), 2.

3. Langley, *Elements of Machine Learning*, 2.

4. Jude W. Shavlik and Thomas G. Dietterich, eds., *Readings in Machine Learning* (San Francisco: Morgan Kaufmann, 1990), 3.

5. Nils J. Nilsson, "Introduction to Machine Learning," 1996, at robotics .stanford.edu/people/nilsson/mlbook.html (accessed September 23, 2004).

6. Langley, *Elements of Machine Learning*, 3.

7. Shavlik and Dietterich, eds., *Readings in Machine Learning*, 3.

8. Leslie Kaelbling, interview by author, August 25, 2004.

9. Langley, *Elements of Machine Learning*, 3.

10. Nilsson, *Introduction to Machine Learning*, 4.

11. Nilsson, *Introduction to Machine Learning*, 3–4.

12. Pat Langley, "Editorial: On Machine Learning," *Machine Learning* 1, no. 1 (March 1986): 7.

13. Peter Reimann and Hans Spada, eds., *Learning in Humans and Machines* (Oxford, UK: Pergamon, 1995), 4–5.

14. "American Association for Artificial Intelligence," 2006, at www.aaai.org (accessed September 24, 2004).

15. Institute for Scientific Information, *Journal Citation Reports* (Philadelphia: Thomson ISI, 2003).

16. Reimann and Spada, eds., *Learning in Humans and Machines*, 4–5.

17. Langley, *Elements of Machine Learning*.

18. Shavlik and Dietterich, eds., *Readings in Machine Learning*.

19. CiteSeer IST Scientific Literature Digital Library, "About CiteSeer," 2004, at citeseer.ist.psu.edu/citeseer.html (accessed September 27, 2004).

20. David Burghes and Alexander Graham, *Introduction to Control Theory, Including Optimal Control* (Chichester, UK: Halstead, 1980).

21. Leslie Pack Kaelbling, Michael L. Littman, and Andrew W. Moore, "Reinforcement Learning: A Survey," *Journal of Artificial Intelligence Research* 4 (May 1996): 237–85.

22. Ephraim Suhir, "Crossing the Lines, or Should We Just Mind Our Own Business?" *Mechanical Engineering* 126, no. 9, (September 2004): 39.

Index

About the Editors
and Contributors

The late **Linda G. Ackerson** was associate professor of library administration and assistant engineering librarian at the University of Illinois at Urbana-Champaign. She received her B.S. in 1977 and M.L.S. in 1990, both from the University of Alabama. She accepted her current position at the Grainger Engineering Library Information Center at the University of Illinois in 1998 and was awarded tenure in 2004. Professor Ackerson provided reference and research assistance and library instruction to the university community and selected and acquired library materials for the Engineering Library.

Prior to joining the University of Illinois, Professor Ackerson was science and engineering reference librarian and assistant professor at the Rodgers Library for Science and Engineering at the University of Alabama from 1991 to 1998. She was the library liaison to the Departments of Biological Sciences, Geology, Electrical Engineering, and Metallurgical Engineering. From 1996 to 1998, she taught *Information Resources: Science and Technology* for the University of Alabama School of Library and Information Studies.

Professor Ackerson was a member of the American Association for Engineering Education and the American Library Association, Association of College and Research Libraries section. Her research and publication record include the evaluation of library collections for multiple disciplinary research.

Steven Baumgart (sbaumgart@library.wisc.edu) is the coordinator of library instruction at the University of Wisconsin, Madison for Memorial Library. He has been the instruction coordinator, reference coordinator, and digital reference coordinator at Loyola University Chicago's Science Library. During his time at Loyola, he was the liaison and bibliographer for the Biology Department.

Anna Berkes (berkesa@monticello.org) earned her B.A. in German studies from Pennsylvania State University in 2002 and worked as a graduate assistant at the Grainger Engineering Library Information Center while working toward her M.L.S. at the University of Illinois at Urbana-Champaign. Since earning her M.L.S. in 2004, she has been employed as the research librarian at the Jefferson Library at Monticello, outside Charlottesville, Virginia.

Teresa U. Berry (Teresa-Berry@utk.edu) is science librarian and associate professor at the University of Tennessee. She received a B.S. with a major in chemistry from the University of Georgia and an M.S.L.S. from the University of Tennessee. She is a member of the Science and Technology section of the Association for College and Research Libraries and has served as co-moderator for the section's listserv, STS-L. She was a contributor to *Notable Women in the Physical Sciences* and has written numerous book reviews for *Library Journal* and *American Reference Books Annual*. In 2005, she was named *Library Journal* Reviewer of the Year for Reference.

Tracy Gabridge (tag@mit.edu) is associate head librarian of the Massachusetts Institute of Technology Barker Engineering Library. She also is a subject specialist serving the Department of Electrical Engineering and Computer Science. Before obtaining her M.L.I.S. degree from the University of Illinois at Urbana-Champaign, Tracy was an engineer and operations manager in the telecommunications industry.

Ron Gilmour (gilmour@lib.utk.edu) is associate professor and technology coordinator at the University of Tennessee. Previously, he served as a science reference librarian at the University of Albany. He is a member of the Science and Technology Section (STS) of the Association of College and Research Libraries and currently serves on the STS Publications Committee.

In addition to his work in science and technology librarianship, Professor Gilmour teaches workshops on Extensible Markup Language for the Library Information Technology Association.

Professor Gilmour obtained his M.L.S. from the University of North Carolina at Chapel Hill, where he also completed a master's degree in biology. His graduate research in biology involved the study of fossil plants from the Lower Devonian of Gaspé, Quebec.

Lura Joseph (luraj@uiuc.edu) is assistant professor of library administration at the University of Illinois at Urbana-Champaign and is geology and digital projects librarian. She was formally associated with Quaternary researchers for fifteen years and has master's degrees in geology and library and information studies from the University of Oklahoma.

Carla H. Lee (cl9eb@virginia.edu) is the coordinator of collections and digital services at the Charles L. Brown Science and Engineering Library at the University of Virginia. Previously, she served as the head of the Science Library at the Loyola University of Chicago. She received her M.L.I.S. from the University of Michigan and a B.A. from Michigan State University. Carla is a member of the American Society for Information Science and Technology and the Special Libraries Administration, where she is a member of the Biomedical and Life Sciences and Sci-Tech divisions. She has written numerous reviews for *E-STREAMS* (www.e-streams.com) and has served as a volunteer abstracter for *ABC-CLIO*.

Meris Mandernach (mmander@luc.edu) is currently a reference/instruction librarian at the Cudahy Library at Loyola University Chicago. She had been the instruction coordinator at Loyola University Chicago's Science Library. While at Loyola, she has served as the liaison and bibliographer for the Chemistry and Natural Sciences Departments.

Kevin Messner (messn006@tc.umn.edu) is assistant science librarian at the Bio-Medical Library and Magrath Library, University of Minnesota Twin Cities. He is the University of Minnesota's liaison and specialist librarian for the molecular biosciences and computational biology. He holds an M.S. in library and information science and a Ph.D. in microbiology, both from the University of Illinois at Urbana-Champaign. He teaches the workshop *Introduction to Molecular Biology and Information Resources* regionally for the National Center for Biotechnology Information and is an active member of the Medical Library Association Molecular Biology Special Interest Group.

Yoo-Seong Song (yoosong@cba.uiuc.edu) is labor and industrial relations librarian and assistant professor of library administration at the University of Illinois at Urbana-Champaign. Prior to coming to the University of Illinois, he had been a business researcher and market analyst at Accenture and Ernst & Young. His research specialization included telecommunications, e-commerce, and technology. He also worked as a competitive intelligence analyst at a global telecommunications equipment company.

He is now a member of the Special Library Association and American Library Association. At the University of Illinois, Professor Song provides business research services and also teaches a course on business information services to graduate library school students. His recent research interests include information-seeking behavior of business students and library marketing. He was awarded the Highly Commended Paper award by Emerald Publishing in 2005.

Jeanine Williamson (jwilliamson@utk.edu) is the engineering librarian and assistant professor at the University of Tennessee. Previously, she served as physical sciences and engineering librarian at the University of Rhode Island. She is a member of the American Society for Engineering Education and the Science and Technology section of the Association of College and Research Libraries.

Professor Williamson received the Association of College and Research Libraries Doctoral Dissertation Award in 1998. Previous publications include papers on librarians and personality in *Reference Librarian, Issues in Science and Technology Libraries*, and *Library Quarterly*.

Gregory Youngen (youngen@uiuc.edu) is presently veterinary medicine librarian and associate professor at the University of Illinois at Urbana-Champaign, having previously served for nine years as the physics/astronomy librarian at the University of Illinois. He also teaches sci/tech information courses at the University of Illinois Graduate School of Library and Information Science as an adjunct professor. Prior to his positions at Illinois, Professor Youngen worked as a technical librarian for the U.S. Department of Energy programs at Oak Ridge National Laboratory and Argonne National Laboratory.

Professor Youngen is a 1983 graduate of the Indiana University School of Library and Information Science and did his undergraduate work at Indiana State University in Terre Haute. He is a member of the Medical Libraries Association and a representative to the Science and Technology Library section of the International Federation of Library Associations.